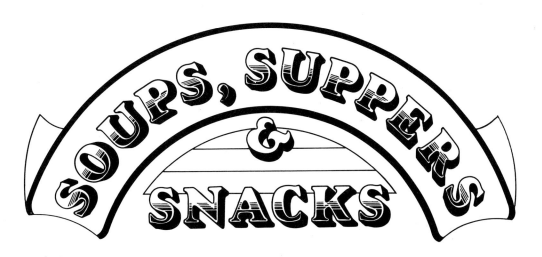

SOUPS, SUPPERS & SNACKS

SOUPS, SUPPERS & SNACKS

Marshall Cavendish

SYMBOLS

 TIME
Timing explained
including preparation
in advance

 SUPERQUICK
Dishes that are
cooked within 1 hour

 FREEZING
The essential guide to
dishes which freeze

 ECONOMY
Tips to make dishes go
further, or for inexpen-
sive ingredients

 WATCHPOINT
Look out for special
advice on tricky methods

 DID YOU KNOW
Useful background to
recipes or ingredients

 PREPARATION
Tips for techniques,
often with illustrations

 SERVING IDEAS
Suggestions for good
accompaniments

 **SPECIAL
OCCASIONS**
Ideas to lift a dish
out of the ordinary

 VARIATIONS
How to ring the changes
on the basic dish

 COOK'S TIPS
Background
information to help
when you need it

 BUYING GUIDE
Guide to selecting
suitable ingredients

Editor: *Miranda Spicer*
Designer: *Johnny Pau*

Published by Marshall Cavendish Books Limited
58 Old Compton Street
London W1V 5PA

© Marshall Cavendish Limited 1986

ISBN 0 86307 440 5

Printed and bound in Hong Kong by
Dai Nippon Printing Company

CONTENTS

INTRODUCTION

To have a cookery book full of variety and colour is an inspiration to any cook. This book gives you the flexibility to combine soups with suppers or snacks and the recipes show you just how easy it is to prepare light meals successfully.

Soup, appropriate whatever the occasion or time of year, is extremely versatile. Ranging from thick and meaty, puréed and creamy to clear and light, it can be based on vegetables, pulses or seafood. Warming and wholesome winter soups give way to refreshingly chilled summer flavours. Soup can be served as a starter or, with fresh bread and salad, becomes a filling meal in itself.

Coming home to supper in the evening is something to look forward to. Quick meals are also ideal when unexpected guests arrive and need to be catered for at short notice. The summer recipes chosen here have been purposely divided into those with and without meat; the vegetable dishes are to be found in the second half of the chapter. This leaves the choice wide for vegetarian meal planning and highlights the advantages of making the most of vegetables, which need not be confined to the role of accompaniment.

The third and final section of the book is full of appetizing snacks, welcome at any time of day. Here, too, there is an array of delicious vegetarian alternatives including both classic and new ideas. Each recipe is calorie-counted so that if you or a member of the family is on a calorie-controlled diet it is possible to stick to it yet still enjoy good food.

All the recipes in *Soups, Suppers and Snacks* are illustrated with full colour photographs to show you how good the finished dish will look on the table. A panel of Cook's Notes accompanies each recipe with advice on preparing, timing and presenting and also indicating which dishes are suitable for the freezer. Most of the recipes call for everyday ingredients, and the techniques are certainly straightforward, so you are sure to be delighted with our superb selection and mouth-watering results.

Soups

The soups in this section are easy to make,
and include popular favourites like mushroom and beef that are
designed to give you the full flavour of home-made cooking.
They can be served either as a first course,
or the more substantial soups can be served
as a lunch or supper dish

Autumn soup

SERVES 4-6

1 large onion, chopped
2 carrots, cut into 1 cm/½ inch dice
1 small swede, cut into 1 cm/½ inch dice
½ green pepper, deseeded and thinly sliced
3 tablespoons vegetable oil
1 tablespoon tomato purée
1 L/1¾ pints beef stock
50 g/2 oz red lentils
salt and freshly ground black pepper
175 g/6 oz pork sausagemeat
25 g/1 oz fresh white breadcrumbs
½ teaspoon chopped fresh rosemary, or 1 teaspoon dried rosemary
1 cooking apple
1 large potato, cut into 1 cm/½ inch dice
snipped chives, to garnish

1 Heat the oil in a large flameproof casserole. Add the onion, carrots, swede and green pepper and fry gently for 3 minutes until the vegetables are soft but not coloured.
2 Stir in the tomato purée, stock and lentils, and season to taste with salt and pepper.
3 Bring to the boil, then lower the heat, cover and simmer for 20 minutes until the vegetables are just tender.
4 Meanwhile, put the sausagemeat, breadcrumbs and rosemary in a bowl. Mix thoroughly with your hands, then shape into 12 small balls.
5 Peel and core the apple, then cut into 1 cm/½ inch dice. Add to the soup with the potato and sausagemeat balls and simmer for a further 25 minutes until all the vegetables are tender.
6 Taste and adjust seasoning, then serve hot, sprinkled with chives.

Cook's Notes

 TIME
Preparation takes 20 minutes, cooking 50 minutes.

 SERVING IDEAS
Serve with crusty bread or rolls as a main-meal soup for lunch. Sprinkle with grated cheese, if liked.

 VARIATIONS
In place of the sausage-meat balls, dice 75 g/3 oz skinned garlic sausage or salami and stir into the soup 10 minutes before the end of cooking. Pearl barley can be used instead of lentils, but you will need to allow at least another 30 minutes cooking time before adding the sausagemeat balls.

 COOK'S TIP
To give the sausage-meat balls a golden-brown colour fry them separately in a little oil, then add to the soup just before serving.

●380 calories/1575 kj per portion

Bean and vegetable soup

SERVES 4

 250 g/9 oz dried haricot beans,
    soaked overnight and drained
 1 tablespoon vegetable oil
    1 large onion, chopped
 2 rashers streaky bacon, rinds
    removed, chopped
2 leeks, chopped
3 celery stalks, chopped
2 carrots, sliced
2 cloves garlic, crushed (optional)
700 ml/1¼ pints chicken stock
225 g/8 oz can tomatoes
1 teaspoon dried oregano
salt and freshly ground black pepper
2 tablespoons chopped parsley, to
    garnish

1 Cover the beans with fresh hot water and boil for 10 minutes, then cover and simmer for about 2 hours until they are tender. Drain.

2 Heat the oil in a large saucepan, add onion and bacon and fry for 2 minutes. Add the leeks, celery and carrots to pan with garlic, if using, and cook a further 2 minutes.

3 Add the stock and beans, together with the tomatoes and their juice, the oregano and plenty of salt and pepper. Bring to the boil, then lower the heat, cover and simmer for 30 minutes until the vegetables are tender. ✳ Sprinkle with parsley.

Cook's Notes

TIME
Preparation takes 15 minutes, cooking time is 2¾ hours.

SERVING IDEAS
Serve the soup with plenty of hot, crusty French bread.

VARIATIONS
Other varieties of dried beans may be used, such as red kidney, black-eye or butter beans. The same cooking instructions apply. Or use canned beans and start the recipe at stage 2.

FREEZING
After stage 3, cool the soup and pour into a rigid container. Seal, label and freeze for up to 3 months.
To defrost: reheat slowly in a pan, stirring from time to time and add seasoning and stock if required.

●285 calories/1200 kj per portion

10

Celery and Stilton soup

SERVES 4

1 head celery (see Cook's tip), finely
   chopped

100 g/4 oz Stilton cheese (see
   Variation), trimmed of rind
40 g/1½ oz butter
2 large leeks, thinly sliced
700 ml/1¼ pints chicken or
   vegetable stock
2 large egg yolks
50 ml/2 fl oz single cream
salt and freshly ground black pepper

Cook's Notes

TIME
Preparation time takes
about 65 minutes.

COOK'S TIP
Save the best leaves
from the celery and add
them to the pan with the
chopped stalks—they give extra
flavour. Reserve a few feathery
ones from the inner stalks for a
garnish, if wished.

VARIATION
Use another type of blue
cheese and adjust the
quantity according to its
strength or mildness of flavour.

WATCHPOINT
Do not let the soup boil,
or the egg and cream
mixture will scramble.

SERVING IDEAS
Garnish each bowl with
chopped fresh parsley,
butter-fried croûtons or celery
leaves. Serve with baps or
granary rolls.

●285 calories/1200 kj per portion

1 Melt the butter in a large, heavy-based saucepan. Add the celery and leeks, cover and cook gently, stirring occasionally, for about 10 minutes, until the vegetables are softened but not coloured.
2 Add the stock and bring to the boil. Lower the heat and simmer, uncovered, for about 20 minutes, until vegetables are tender. Cool slightly, then work to a puree in a blender.
3 Return the soup to the rinsed-out pan and reheat gently, without bringing to the boil.
4 Meanwhile, beat the egg yolks and cream together until smoothly blended. In a separate bowl, mash the cheese to a coarse paste with a fork, then gradually work in the egg and cream mixture.
5 Stir a small ladleful of the hot soup into the cheese mixture, then pour the mixture back into the pan, stirring constantly until the soup has thickened slightly. ⚠ Serve at once, in warmed individual bowls (see Serving ideas).

Creamy mushroom soup

SERVES 4

250 g/9 oz button mushrooms (see
   Buying guide)
50 g/2 oz butter
2 tablespoons plain flour
600 ml/1 pint milk
75 g/3 oz full-fat soft
   cheese with chives
2 teaspoons lemon juice
salt and freshly ground black pepper
1 tablespoon snipped chives, to
   garnish

Cook's Notes

TIME
Making the soup takes
only 25 minutes.

BUYING GUIDE
Choose small button or
cup mushrooms for this
recipe. Their delicate flavour
blends well with the soft
cheese. There is no need to peel
them before using.
   The larger open mushrooms
may be used but the flavour will
be stronger and the colour
slightly darker.

VARIATION
This is a thick creamy
soup; if you prefer a
thinner soup use only 1 tablespoon flour and replace 300ml/
½ pint milk with a well-
flavoured chicken stock.

WATCHPOINT
Take care not to boil the
soup after adding the
cheese and mushrooms or it
may spoil the flavour.

● 270 calories/1125 kj per serving

1 Finely chop the mushrooms,
reserving 2-3 whole ones for the
garnish. Melt half the butter in a
frying-pan. Add the chopped
mushrooms and fry gently for about
5 minutes until soft. Set aside.
2 Melt the remaining butter in a
large saucepan, sprinkle in flour and
stir over low heat for 1-2 minutes
until it is straw-coloured. Remove
from the heat and gradually stir
in milk. Return to the heat and
simmer, stirring, until the mixture
is thick and smooth.
3 Remove from the heat, add the
cheese a little at a time and stir until
melted. Stir in the mushrooms,
their juices and the lemon juice.
Season to taste. Return to heat and
simmer for 2-3 minutes.
4 Pour into 4 warmed soup bowls.
Float a few slices of mushrooms on
top of each serving. Sprinkle lightly
with chives and serve at once.

Cream of chestnut soup

SERVES 4-6

750 g/1½ lb fresh chestnuts
1.25 L/2 pints chicken stock
1 bay leaf
2 onions, sliced
about 150 ml/¼ pint milk
1 egg yolk
150 ml/¼ pint whipping cream
pinch of freshly grated nutmeg
salt and freshly ground black pepper
1-2 teaspoons sugar

Cook's Notes

TIME
Preparation takes 45-60 minutes (peeling the chestnuts is a lengthy process). Cooking 1½ hours, blending and finishing the soup, 15 minutes.

SERVING IDEAS
This is a substantial soup, ideal to serve on cold days with chunky slices of wholemeal bread and butter and wedges of cheese.

COOK'S TIP
Keeping the chestnuts in hot water makes them easier to peel. If they are drained the skins toughen.

WATCHPOINT
Take care not to boil the soup at this stage as the egg and cream may overheat and curdle, and spoil the appearance of the dish.

●460 calories/1925 kj per portion

1 Nick the chestnuts with a sharp knife, then place in a saucepan and cover with cold water. Gradually bring to the boil and simmer for 10 minutes.

2 Remove the pan from the heat, then take out the chestnuts, a few at a time (see Cook's tip). Remove both the outside and inside skins.

3 Put the peeled chestnuts into a large pan together with the chicken stock, bay leaf and onions. Bring to the boil, then lower the heat, cover and simmer gently for 1½ hours.

4 Remove the bay leaf, then press the soup through a sieve or work in a blender.

5 Return the soup to the rinsed-out pan and gradually stir in enough milk to make it a smooth consistency. Heat through gently. Blend the egg yolk and cream in a bowl. Remove the pan from the heat and stir in the egg and cream. Reheat if necessary, but do not boil. !

6 Add the nutmeg, and season to taste with salt and pepper. Add the sugar, a little at a time, to taste. Pour into warmed individual soup bowls and serve at once.

Lentil and lemon soup

SERVES 4
100 g/4 oz split red lentils
15 g/½ oz margarine or butter
2 celery stalks, chopped
1 medium onion, finely chopped
1 L/1¾ pints boiling water
2 chicken stock cubes
grated zest and juice of 1 lemon
¼ teaspoon ground cumin
   (optional)
salt and freshly ground black pepper
1 red pepper, deseeded and thinly
   sliced into rings

TO GARNISH
1 lemon, thinly sliced
snipped chives (optional)

1 Melt the margarine in a saucepan,
add the celery and onion, then cover
and cook gently for 4 minutes.
2 Remove the pan from the heat,
then stir in the lentils and water,
with the stock cubes. Add the lemon
zest and juice, and the cumin, if
using. Season to taste with salt and
pepper. Cover and simmer over
very gentle heat for 30 minutes.
3 Add the sliced pepper to the pan,
cover and cook for a further 30
minutes. Taste and adjust
seasoning. ✳
4 Pour the soup into warmed
serving bowls, float the lemon slices
on top, then sprinkle over the
chives, if using. Serve at once.

Cook's Notes

TIME
Preparation 20 minutes;
cooking takes 65
minutes.

FREEZING
Cool quickly, then freeze
without the lemon
and chives in a rigid polythene
container or freezer bag (do not
use foil containers, or the acid in
the soup may react against the
foil). Seal, label and freeze for
up to 6 months. Defrost at room
temperature, then reheat until
bubbling, adding a little more
water if necessary.

SERVING IDEAS
Warm crusty rolls are
ideal to serve with this
soup. For a luxurious touch, top
each serving with 1 tablespoon
soured cream.

VARIATIONS
For a lentil and orange
soup, use 2 small oranges
instead of lemons.
   If chives are unavailable, use
chopped spring onion tops or
parsley, if using another
garnish as well as the lemon.

●135 calories/550 kj per portion

Scotch broth

SERVES 4-6

25 g/1 oz pearl barley
225 g/8 oz stewing steak or mutton, finely diced
1.25 L/2 pints cold water
100 g/4 oz leeks, sliced
250 g/9 oz carrots, diced
250 g/9 oz swede, diced
salt and freshly ground black pepper
50 g/2 oz green cabbage, sliced
2-3 tablespoons freshly chopped parsley

1 Blanch the barley: place it in a medium-sized saucepan half-filled with water, bring to boil and drain.
2 Put the barley and meat in a large saucepan and pour in the water. Bring slowly to the boil, then lower the heat, cover and simmer for 1 hour. Skim off any excess fat with a slotted spoon.
3 Add the leeks, carrots and swede and season with salt and pepper. Cover pan again and simmer liquid gently for another 1½ hours.
4 Add the cabbage and cook for a further 10 minutes. Skim again to remove any more excess fat (see Cook's tip) then taste and adjust seasoning, if necessary. Serve in warmed bowls, sprinkling each serving very generously with parsley.

Fish and vegetable soup

SERVES 4

225 g/8 oz cod steaks, defrosted if frozen, bones and skin removed and cut into 2 cm/¾ inch pieces
1 tablespoon vegetable oil
1 small onion, chopped
2 potatoes, cut into 1 cm/½ inch dice (see Buying guide)
2 carrots, cut into 1 cm/½ inch dice
25 g/1 oz plain flour
300 ml/½ pint warm milk
600 ml/1 pint warm chicken stock
1 bay leaf
salt and freshly ground black pepper
50 g/2 oz peeled prawns
½ bunch watercress, stalks removed, to garnish

1 Heat the oil in a large saucepan, add the onion, potatoes and carrots and cook over gentle heat, stirring, for 3 minutes.
2 Sprinkle in the flour, stir for 1 minute, then remove from heat and gradually stir in the milk and stock.
3 Return the pan to the heat and bring to boil, stirring. Lower heat, add bay leaf and salt and pepper to taste. Simmer for 15 minutes.
4 Add the cod to the pan and simmer for a further 10 minutes.
5 Discard the bay leaf, stir the prawns into the soup and heat through for 5 minutes. ✳ Taste and adjust seasoning, then pour into warmed individual soup bowls and garnish with the watercress. Serve the soup at once.

Cook's Notes

 TIME
Preparation takes 20 minutes and cooking about 35 minutes.

 FREEZING
Make the soup without adding the watercress. Cool quickly, then freeze in a polythene bag or rigid container for up to 3 months. Reheat from frozen, adding a little extra milk or stock if liked.

VARIATIONS
Any white fish may be used instead of cod.
Use 2 tablespoons chopped parsley or snipped chives instead of the watercress.
Swirl 1 tablespoon top of the milk or cream on top of each bowl just before serving.

WATCHPOINT
Do not allow the vegetables to brown, or the soup will be light brown instead of pale and creamy.

BUYING GUIDE
Choose floury potatoes such as King Edward. Waxy potatoes are not suitable for making soups, as they do not disintegrate so easily.

●250 calories/1050 kj per portion

Mussel soup

SERVES 4

2 kg/4½ lb fresh mussels (see
    Buying guide and Preparation)
2 tablespoons vegetable oil
25 g/1 oz butter
1 large onion, finely chopped
1 clove garlic, crushed (optional)
3 tablespoons finely chopped fresh
    coriander (see Variation)
700 ml/1¼ pints water
150 ml/¼ pint white wine
225 g/8 oz can tomatoes, drained
    and chopped
salt and freshly ground black pepper

1 Heat the oil and butter in a large
heavy-based saucepan, add the
onion, the garlic, if using, and the
coriander and fry gently for about
5 minutes until the onion is soft
and lightly coloured.
2 Pour in the water and wine and
add the tomatoes. Season to taste
with salt and pepper.

3 Add the mussels and bring to the
boil. Cover the pan, lower the heat
and simmer gently for about 10
minutes or until the mussel shells
have opened. Discard any mussels
that do not open during cooking.
4 Spoon the mussels and soup into
a warmed soup tureen or individual
soup bowls and serve at once (see
Serving ideas).

Cook's Notes

 TIME
Preparing and cooking
the soup takes about 30
minutes. Allow extra time for
preparing the mussels.

 PREPARATION
Check that the mussels
are fresh: tap any open
ones against a work surface and
discard if they do not shut. Pull
away any beards (pieces of
seaweed) gripped between the
shells of the mussels. Scrub the
mussels under cold running
water, then scrape away the
encrustations with a sharp
knife. Soak the mussels in fresh
cold water to cover for 2-3 hours,
changing the water several
times during this period.

 BUYING GUIDE
Fresh mussels are
available from October-
March. Always buy them the
day you are going to eat them.
Look for closed mussels with
unbroken shells. Frozen shelled
mussels, which are available all
year round, can be used instead.

 VARIATION
Use parsley or chervil
instead of coriander.

 SERVING IDEAS
The mussels can be
eaten with the fingers
so provide napkins and a large
dish to put the empty shells in.

●255 calories/1050 kj per portion

Sweetcorn and tuna chowder

SERVES 4-6

 350 g/12 oz can sweetcorn
200 g/7 oz can tuna
 25 g/1 oz margarine or butter
1 large onion, finely chopped
2 tablespoons plain flour
2 teaspoons sweet paprika
pinch of cayenne pepper
850 ml/1½ pints milk
pinch of salt
grated zest of ½ lemon

TO FINISH
50 g/2 oz Cheddar cheese, finely
   grated
4 tablespoons chopped parsley

1 Drain the sweetcorn, reserving the juice. Drain off the oil from the tuna fish and discard. Place the fish on absorbent paper to remove excess oil. Flake the fish into a bowl.

2 Melt the margarine in a saucepan, add the onion and cook gently until soft but not coloured.
3 Stir in the flour, paprika and cayenne pepper and cook for 1 minute, stirring constantly with a wooden spoon. Gradually stir in 300 ml/½ pint milk and the reserved sweetcorn juice and bring to the boil, stirring.
4 Stir in the remaining milk and bring the mixture to simmering point. Add the salt and the grated lemon zest.
5 Add the sweetcorn and simmer the soup, uncovered, for 5 minutes. Add the tuna fish and simmer for a further 5 minutes until heated through.
6 To finish: taste and adjust seasoning, then pour into warmed individual soup bowls. Sprinkle with the cheese and parsley and serve at once.

Cook's Notes

TIME
The soup takes 30 minutes to prepare and cook.

COOK'S TIP
To make the soup in advance, prepare it up to the end of stage 4, leave to cool, then refrigerate. To finish: re-heat until bubbling, stirring constantly, then continue from stage 5.

WATCHPOINT
It is important to re-move as much oil as possible from the tuna so that the chowder is not greasy.
Always add the cheese just before serving, when the soup is still hot enough for it to melt. Do not bring back to the boil after adding the cheese or the soup will be stringy.

● 410 calories/1725 kj per portion

Provençal fish chowder

SERVES 4-6

750 g/1½ lb coley fillets, skinned
    and cut into 4 cm/1½ inch pieces
    (see Variation)
3 tablespoons vegetable oil
500 g/1 lb onions, grated
850 g/28 oz can tomatoes
bouquet garni
2 potatoes, cut into 1 cm/½ inch
    cubes
24 small black olives, halved and
    stoned
2 tablespoons capers, drained
300 ml/½ pint tomato juice
600 ml/1 pint vegetable stock (see
    Preparation)
salt and freshly ground black pepper
3 tablespoons finely chopped fresh
    parsley

1 Heat the oil in a large saucepan, add the onions and fry gently for 5 minutes until soft and lightly coloured. Add the tomatoes, with their juice, and the bouquet garni. Bring to the boil, then lower the heat and simmer for 5 minutes, stirring and breaking up the tomatoes with a wooden spoon.
2 Add all the remaining ingredients except the parsley and simmer uncovered, for 10-15 minutes, or until the potato is cooked (see Cook's tip).
3 Add the fish to the pan and simmer gently, uncovered, for about 5 minutes, or until the fish is tender but not breaking up. Remove the bouquet garni, stir in the parsley, then taste and adjust seasoning. Transfer to a warmed serving bowl and serve at once.

Cook's Notes

 TIME
Total preparation and cooking time is about 50 minutes.

 PREPARATION
For vegetable stock, save the liquid from cooked vegetables such as carrots and cabbage. Alternatively, use a vegetable stock cube, from health food shops.

 **SPECIAL OCCASION**
This chowder is a meal in itself and excellent for an informal lunch or supper party dish. Give it a real Mediterranean flavour by adding a crushed clove of garlic.

 VARIATION
Use cod or haddock fillets as a substitute for the coley.

 COOK'S TIP
You can prepare the chowder up to the end of stage 2 the day before, then add the fish and complete the cooking just before serving.

 SERVING IDEAS
Serve with toasted French bread and butter.

●395 calories/1650 kj per portion

Mushroom soup with dumplings

SERVES 4

250 g/9 oz flat mushrooms, finely chopped
295 g/10½ oz can condensed consommé
700 ml/1¼ pints cold water
1 onion, finely chopped
bouquet garni
salt and freshly ground black pepper
chopped fresh parsley, to garnish (optional)

DUMPLINGS

75 g/3 oz self-raising flour
40 g/1½ oz shredded suet
½ teaspoon salt
1-2 tablespoons finely chopped fresh parsley
2-3 tablespoons cold water

1 Put the consommé into a saucepan and stir in the water. Add the chopped mushrooms, onion, and bouquet garni and season to taste with salt and pepper. ! Bring to the boil, then lower the heat, cover and simmer for 10 minutes, stirring occasionally.

2 Meanwhile, stir all the dry dumpling ingredients together in a bowl. Mix to form a soft but not sticky dough with the cold water. Shape into 12-16 small balls with your hands.

3 Drop the dumplings into the soup, bring back to the boil, then lower the heat again and simmer for a further 15 minutes until the dumplings are cooked through.

4 To serve: remove the bouquet garni and pour the soup into warmed individual soup bowls. Add a few dumplings to each bowl, then sprinkle with a little chopped parsley, if wished.

Cook's Notes

TIME
The soup takes about 35 minutes to make.

WATCHPOINT
Add salt sparingly because canned consommé tends to have a salty flavour.

SERVING IDEAS
Serve this soup as a filling starter before a light lunch or dinner.

VARIATION
Substitute the parsley in the dumplings with ½ teaspoon dried mixed herbs or caraway seeds.

● 170 calories/725 kj per portion

Frankfurter and vegetable soup

SERVES 4

100 g/4 oz frankfurters, cut into 5 mm/¼ inch slices
2 tablespoons vegetable oil
175 g/6 oz carrots, cut into 1 cm/½ inch dice
1 celery stalk, thinly sliced
250 g/9 oz turnips, cut into 1 cm/½ inch dice
1 onion, chopped
1 clove garlic, crushed (optional)
700 ml/1¼ pints beef stock
400 g/14 oz can chopped tomatoes
salt and freshly ground black pepper
50 g/2 oz green cabbage leaves, shredded
25 g/1 oz pasta (see Buying guide)
50 g/2 oz Cheddar cheese, grated

1 Heat the oil in a heavy-based saucepan, add the carrots, celery, turnips, onion and garlic, if using, and cook over moderate heat for 7 minutes, stirring.

2 Remove from the heat and stir in the stock and tomatoes. Season to taste with salt and pepper.
3 Return the pan to the heat and bring to the boil. Lower the heat, cover the pan and simmer for 20 minutes.
4 Add the cabbage and pasta, then cover again and simmer for a further 10 minutes until the pasta is soft.
5 Stir in the frankfurters, taste and adjust seasoning, and cook for a further 3 minutes.
6 Ladle into warmed individual bowls or a soup tureen and serve at once. Hand the grated cheese in a separate bowl for sprinkling on top of the soup.

Cook's Notes

 TIME
Preparation takes 20 minutes, cooking 45 minutes.

 BUYING GUIDE
Soup pasta, or pastina, as the Italians call it, comes in tiny star and circle shapes. If it is not available, use small pasta shapes or quick-cook pasta broken into 1 cm/½ inch lengths.

 VARIATION
Use potatoes or swedes in place of turnips.

FREEZING
Transfer to a rigid container, cool quickly, then seal, label and freeze for up to 6 months. To serve: defrost at room temperature for 2-3 hours, then reheat thoroughly until bubbling.
Add a little more stock if necessary.

SERVING IDEAS
Serve this hearty soup with toast or wholemeal bread for a meal in itself.

●250 calories/1060 kj per portion

Green pepper cream soup

SERVES 4

250 g/9 oz green peppers, deseeded (see Watchpoint)

25 g/1 oz margarine or butter

1 large onion, chopped

1 clove garlic, chopped (see Cook's tip)

15 g/½ oz plain flour

600 ml/1 pint chicken stock

1 teaspoon chopped fresh herbs, or ½ teaspoon dried mixed herbs

salt and freshly ground black pepper

1 teaspoon lemon juice

150 ml/¼ pint single cream (see Economy)

Cook's Notes

TIME
This soup takes about 35 minutes to make.

WATCHPOINT
Use green peppers only for this soup. Red peppers are sweeter than the green ones, but will give an entirely different, less pleasant flavour and colour.

COOK'S TIP
Even if you do not usually use garlic, it is worth including in this soup: the flavour is subtle rather than obvious.

SERVING IDEAS
Serve the soup with bread and cheese to make a nutritious supper, or with fingers of wholemeal toast and butter for a snack or dinner-party starter.

ECONOMY
Evaporated milk can be used instead of single cream. It is far less expensive than single cream and its stronger flavour combines very successfully with the green peppers.

●170 calories/715 kj per portion

1 Cut a few very thin rings from one of the peppers and set aside for garnish. Chop the remainder.

2 Melt the margarine in a heavy-based saucepan. Add the chopped peppers, onion and garlic and cook over very low heat for about 10 minutes, stirring frequently, until the vegetables are soft but not brown.

3 Sprinkle in the flour and cook for 1-2 minutes, stirring, then gradually stir in the stock. Add the herbs, and season to taste with salt and pepper. Cover and cook gently for 20-25 minutes until the vegetables are tender.

4 Leave to cool slightly, then transfer to a blender and blend for about 5 seconds until smooth. If you do not have a blender, work the vegetables through a sieve while still hot. Return the soup to the rinsed-out pan, add lemon juice and cream, then taste and adjust seasoning if necessary. Heat through thoroughly, but do not boil.

5 Serve hot, garnished with the reserved pepper rings.

Leekie oat broth

SERVES 4

100 g/4 oz leeks, thinly sliced
600 ml/1 pint chicken stock
100 g/4 oz carrots, finely chopped
½ teaspoon dried mixed herbs
salt and freshly ground black pepper
25 g/1 oz porridge oats (see Cook's tip)
150 ml/¼ pint milk
2 tablespoons single cream or evaporated milk
100 g/4 oz Edam cheese, cubed, to serve

1 Pour the stock into a saucepan and bring to the boil. Add the leeks, carrots, herbs and salt and pepper to taste. Lower the heat, cover and simmer for 15 minutes or until the vegetables are tender.

2 Sprinkle the oats into the soup, stir in the milk and cook gently, uncovered, for 5 minutes, stirring occasionally, until thick. Stir in the cream or evaporated milk and heat through without allowing the soup to boil.

3 To serve: ladle into a warmed tureen or individual serving bowls and mix the cubes of Edam cheese into the soup. Serve at once, before the cheese has completely melted. !

Cauliflower cheese soup

SERVES 4

 250 g/9 oz cauliflower, broken into small florets
50 g/2 oz butter
1 onion, chopped
1 potato, thinly sliced
300 ml/½ pint chicken stock
300 ml/½ pint milk
50 g/2 oz Cheddar cheese, grated
salt and freshly ground black pepper

GARNISH
4 tablespoons single cream
25 g/1 oz Cheddar cheese, grated
1 tablespoon chopped parsley

1 Melt the butter in a large saucepan, add the onion and fry gently for 5 minutes until soft and lightly coloured. Add the cauliflower florets and potato slices. Cover and cook the vegetables for 10 minutes.

2 Stir in the stock, bring to the boil, then cover and simmer for about 25-30 minutes, or until all the vegetables are very soft.

3 Transfer the vegetables and stock to the goblet of a blender and work until smooth. Return the purée to the rinsed-out pan and stir in the milk off the heat.

4 Heat the purée gently until simmering then remove from heat and stir in the grated cheese. Season to taste with salt and pepper.

5 Pour the soup into 4 warmed individual soup bowls and swirl 1 tablespoon cream into each (see Cook's tip). Place a quarter of the cheese on top of each serving and sprinkle over a little chopped parsley. Serve at once.

Cook's Notes

 TIME
Preparation takes 5-10 minutes. Cooking time is 40-45 minutes.

COOK'S TIP
For an attractive finish swirl the cream over the entire surface of the soup in a light feathery pattern, rather than just in a single swirl.

SERVING IDEAS
Serve this very filling soup with Melba toast or crispbread.

●300 calories/1250 kj per portion

Chilled carrot and orange soup

SERVES 4

500 g/1 lb carrots, thinly sliced
1 tablespoon vegetable oil
1 onion, finely chopped
2 tablespoons medium-dry sherry
(optional)
600 ml/1 pint chicken stock
salt and freshly ground black pepper
grated zest of 1 orange
juice of 3 large oranges
1 small carrot, grated, to garnish

Cook's Notes

TIME
15 minutes preparation, 45 minutes cooking, plus 2 hours chilling time.

VARIATION
4 tablespoons unsweetened concentrated orange juice may be substituted for the fresh orange juice.

SERVING IDEAS
If serving the soup at a summer dinner party, give it a special garnish. Cut half an orange into 4 very thin slices. Remove the rind and pith. Float 1 orange slice on top of each bowl of chilled soup and arrange a little grated carrot on top of the slices.

The soup can also be served hot: prepare to stage 3 but do not cool, reduce to a purée at once and reheat gently with the orange zest and juice.

●130 calories/550 kj per portion

1 Heat the oil in a saucepan, add the onion and fry gently for 5 minutes until soft and lightly coloured. Add the sherry, if using, and bring to the boil.
2 Add the sliced carrots and stock to the pan and season to taste.

3 Bring to the boil, stirring, then lower the heat, cover and simmer gently for 45 minutes until the carrots are very tender. Leave to cool.
4 Pass the soup through a sieve or purée in a blender. Pour the soup into a bowl, cover and refrigerate for

at least 2 hours or overnight.
5 Just before serving, stir the orange zest and juice into the soup, then taste and adjust seasoning. Pour into 4 chilled individual soup bowls, sprinkle a little grated carrot on to each bowl and serve at once.

Leek and barley soup

SERVES 4

4 leeks, sliced
50 g/2 oz pearl barley
1 tablespoon vegetable oil
1 small onion, chopped
2 carrots, sliced
400 g/14 oz can tomatoes
600 ml/1 pint vegetable stock or
   water (see Cook's tip)
½ teaspoon dried mixed herbs
1 bay leaf
salt and freshly ground black pepper
215 g/7½ oz can butter beans,
   drained

CHEESY BREAD

4 round slices French bread,
   2 cm/¾ inch thick
40 g/1½ oz butter, for frying
1 clove garlic, cut in half (optional)
100 g/4 oz Cheddar cheese, grated

1 Heat the oil in a large saucepan, add the onion, leeks and carrots and fry gently for 3-4 minutes.

2 Add the tomatoes with their juice, the stock and the barley, herbs and bay leaf. Season to taste with salt and pepper. Bring to the boil, stirring, then lower the heat, cover and simmer for 50 minutes. Stir occasionally during this time.

3 Meanwhile, make the cheesy bread: melt the butter in a frying-pan and when it sizzles add the slices of French bread. Fry over fairly high heat, turning once, until the bread is crisp and golden brown on both sides. Remove from the pan, drain on absorbent paper and leave to cool.

4 Rub each side of fried bread with the cut sides of the garlic, if using. Press the grated cheese evenly on to the slices of bread, dividing it equally between them. Heat the grill to high.

5 Remove the bay leaf from the soup, stir in the drained beans and heat through. Adjust seasoning.

Cook's Notes

TIME
Preparation takes 15 minutes, cooking 1 hour.

COOK'S TIP
Vegetable stock cubes are difficult to obtain, but you may find them in a good continental delicatessen. To make your own vegetable stock, simply use the liquid in which you have cooked vegetables.

FREEZING
Cool the soup quickly after stage 2, discard the bay leaf, then freeze in a rigid container for up to 3 months. To defrost: place the soup in a large saucepan and cook over low heat, stirring from time to time. Make the cheesy bread and add the beans as from the beginning of stage 3.

●340 calories/1425 kj per portion

6 Toast the cheese-topped slices of bread until the cheese starts to bubble.

7 Ladle the soup into 4 warmed individual soup bowls and top each one with a slice of cheesy bread. Serve at once.

26

Cabbage and sausage soup

SERVES 4-6

350 g/12 oz white cabbage, finely shredded
175 g/6 oz cocktail sausages (see Buying guide)
15 g/½ oz butter
1 onion, chopped
250 g/9 oz potatoes, peeled and diced
850 ml/1½ pints chicken stock
1 bay leaf
salt and freshly ground black pepper
pinch of grated nutmeg
3 tablespoons double cream
1 tablespoon fresh chopped parsley, to garnish

1 Melt the butter in a large pan. Add the cabbage, onion, and the potatoes and cook gently, stirring, for about 3 minutes (see Cook's tip).
2 Add the stock, bay leaf and salt, pepper and nutmeg to taste. Bring to the boil, then reduce heat, cover saucepan with a lid and simmer gently for 30 minutes.
3 Meanwhile, heat the grill to medium and grill the sausages for 15 minutes, turning frequently during cooking.
4 Remove the soup from the heat and discard the bay leaf. Cool for a few minutes, then liquidize in a blender or press through a sieve. Return to a clean pan and add the sausages and cream. Heat gently for 5 minutes and adjust seasoning if necessary. Spoon into individual warmed bowls and sprinkle with chopped parsley before serving.

Curried turnip soup

SERVES 4

 500 g/1 lb small turnips, quartered (see Cook's tip)
 salt
25 g/1 oz margarine or butter
1 small onion, finely chopped
2 teaspoons mild curry powder (see Variation)
600 ml/1 pint chicken stock
1 teaspoon sugar
juice of ½ lemon
freshly ground black pepper
150 ml/¼ pint single cream
1 tablespoon finely chopped parsley, to garnish

1 Blanch the turnips by plunging them into a large pan of boiling salted water and simmering for 3 minutes. Drain at once.
2 Melt the margarine in a large saucepan and add the turnips with the onion. Cover the pan and cook for 5 minutes over very gentle heat, shaking the pan occasionally to prevent the vegetables from sticking.

3 Stir in the curry powder, then pour in the stock. Add the sugar and lemon juice and season to taste with salt and pepper. Cover the pan and simmer over low heat for about 10 minutes or until the turnips are soft.
4 Press the turnips and liquid through a sieve, or leave to cool then purée in a blender.
5 Return the turnip purée to the rinsed-out pan and heat through thoroughly. Taste and adjust seasoning then pour immediately into warmed individual soup bowls. Swirl cream into each portion and sprinkle with parsley.

Cook's Notes

 TIME
Preparation takes 10-15 minutes, cooking about 20 minutes.

 COOK'S TIP
Stage 1 can be omitted for new, summer turnips but winter turnips need to be peeled thickly to remove the fibrous matter, and the initial blanching is essential.

 FREEZING
Prepare the soup up to the end of stage 4 (never add the cream before freezing soup). Cool the soup and freeze in a rigid container for up to 1 month. To serve: reheat from frozen, gradually bring to the boil, reduce heat, then add the cream.
Freezing tends to affect the strength of the curry powder, so check the seasoning while you are reheating the soup.

 SERVING IDEAS
Serve with wholemeal bread and cheese for a warming, nourishing supper dish.

 VARIATION
This soup has a mild curry flavour acceptable to most tastes, but the amount of curry powder may be increased to 3 or even 4 teaspoons.

●140 calories/575 kj per portion

Kidney soup with dumplings

SERVES 4

250 g/9 oz lamb kidneys, skinned, cored and finely chopped
75 g/3 oz onion, diced
75 g/3 oz carrot, diced
850 ml/1½ pints chicken stock
½ teaspoon tomato purée
salt and freshly ground black pepper
about 6 tablespoons milk
1-2 tablespoons chopped fresh parsley, to garnish

DUMPLINGS
100 g/4 oz pork sausagemeat
25 g/1 oz plain flour
¼ teaspoon dried mixed herbs
½ teaspoon Worcestershire sauce
½ small egg, beaten

1 Put the kidneys in a large saucepan with the onion, carrot, chicken stock and tomato purée. Season to taste with salt and pepper, bring to the boil, then cover and cook gently for 15-20 minutes.

2 Make the dumplings: put the sausagemeat, flour, herbs, Worcestershire sauce and egg into a bowl and season with salt and pepper. Using a round-bladed knife, work all the ingredients together to make a slightly sticky mixture (see Cook's tips). Divide into 12 equal portions. Lift each dumpling on the knife and add to the soup, keeping them separate. Continue cooking the soup for a further 20 minutes.

3 Using a slotted spoon, lift out the dumplings on to a plate and keep warm while blending soup.

4 Leave the soup to cool slightly then work in a blender until smooth. Return to the pan, stir in enough milk to make a runny consistency, then add the dumplings. Heat through for 2-3 minutes.

5 Transfer the soup and dumplings to 4 warmed soup bowls, sprinkle with parsley and serve at once.

Cook's Notes

TIME
The soup and the dumplings take about 50 minutes to prepare and cook.

SERVING IDEAS
Serve for supper or lunch with chunky slices of bread or split rolls, plain or toasted.

●185 calories/775 kj per portion

COOK'S TIPS
Because the sausage dumplings are a softer texture than ordinary dumplings, they are more easy to handle with a knife than with the fingers.

The soup and dumplings can be prepared in advance, kept in the refrigerator, then reheated for 5-10 minutes over moderate heat when needed.

Vegetable soup

SERVES 4

225 g/8 oz packet frozen mixed
   vegetables
425 ml/¾ pint boiling chicken stock
40 g/1½ oz margarine or butter
1 medium onion, chopped
40 g/1½ oz plain flour
425 ml/¾ pint warm milk
1 tablespoon tomato purée
salt and freshly ground black pepper

CROUTONS

4 tablespoons vegetable oil
4 slices day-old bread, crusts
   removed, cut into small cubes

1 Pour the stock into a saucepan. Add the frozen vegetables and cook gently for 8 minutes.

2 Melt the margarine in a heavy-based saucepan over moderate heat. When the foam subsides, add the onion and fry until golden.

3 Sprinkle in the flour and stir over low heat for 2 minutes until straw-coloured. Remove from the heat and gradually stir in the milk, then return to the heat and simmer, stirring with a wooden spoon until the mixture is thick and smooth. Stir in the tomato purée.

4 Add the mixture to the stock and vegetables, and season with salt and pepper to taste. Stir well and cook gently for 15 minutes, stirring occasionally.

5 To prepare the croûtons: heat the oil in a frying-pan over moderate heat until very hot. Fry the bread cubes until golden brown. [!] Remove from the pan and drain on absorbent paper.

6 Reserve 2 tablespoons vegetables, then blend the remaining ingredients in a blender or rub them through a sieve. Return to the pan, taste and adjust seasoning and heat through until boiling.

7 Pour the soup into heated individual bowls, then stir in the reserved vegetables. Hand the croûtons around separately.

Cook's Notes

TIME
This soup takes 30 minutes to make.

VARIATIONS
Use just one vegetable, such as peas or carrots. For a change leave the soup unblended or blend for only 2 seconds so that the vegetables are only partially chopped.

SERVING IDEAS
To make the soup more substantial, hand round a bowl of grated Parmesan or Cheddar cheese for sprinkling on the soup while it is still piping hot.

[!] WATCHPOINT
Watch the croûtons carefully while they are frying so that they do not burn.

●595 calories/2475 kj per portion

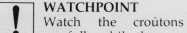

Beefy soup

SERVES 4-6

425 g/15 oz can savoury minced beef
40 g/1½ oz lard
2 onions, finely chopped
1 large potato, cut into 1 cm/½ inch dice
1 large green pepper, deseeded and cut into chunks
2 teaspoons sweet paprika
2 tablespoons tomato purée
850 ml/1½ pints beef stock (see Cook's tip)
200 g/7 oz can sweetcorn, drained
salt and freshly ground black pepper
150 ml/¼ pint soured cream
1 tablespoon snipped chives, to garnish

1 Melt the lard in a large saucepan, add the onions and potato and fry gently for about 5 minutes. Add the green pepper and cook for a further 10 minutes, stirring the vegetables occasionally to prevent them from sticking.
2 Sprinkle the paprika into the pan and cook for 1-2 minutes. Add the tomato purée and minced beef, stirring with a wooden spoon to remove any lumps. Cook for 5 minutes, then pour in the beef stock and bring to the boil. Lower the heat and simmer for about 15 minutes, until the potatoes are tender.
3 Stir in the sweetcorn, heat through for 1-2 minutes, then taste and adjust seasoning if necessary.
4 Pour into warmed individual soup bowls. Top each serving with a swirl of soured cream, sprinkle with the chives and serve at once.

Bread and cheese soup

SERVES 4

 12 × 1 cm/½ inch slices French bread

 225 g/8 oz finely grated Cheddar cheese
40 g/1½ oz butter
175 g/6 oz onions, finely chopped
1 clove garlic, crushed (optional)
450 ml/16 fl oz chicken stock
good pinch grated nutmeg
1 teaspoon Worcestershire sauce
8 teaspoons finely grated Parmesan cheese

1 Melt the butter in a saucepan then add the onions and garlic, if using. Fry over gentle heat for 8-10 minutes until tender and lightly browned.

2 Stir in the stock and season with nutmeg and Worcestershire sauce. Bring to the boil then reduce heat, cover with lid and simmer very gently for 10 minutes. !

3 Heat the oven to 200C/400F/Gas 6.

4 Fill four 300 ml/½ pint ovenproof soup bowls (about 9 cm/3½ inches in diameter) to within about 4 cm/1½ inches of top with alternating layers of French bread and finely grated Cheddar cheese.

5 Gently pour in prepared onion broth so that it only just covers the bread and cheese. Allow to stand for about 5-10 minutes. !

Cook's Notes

TIME
Allow 20 minutes to prepare the onion broth, 15 minutes to assemble the dish and 15-20 minutes to bake the soup in the oven.

SERVING IDEAS
For an attractive supper tray meal, serve this thick, substantial soup with more French bread and butter and follow with fresh fruit.

VARIATIONS
The broth prepared in stages 1 and 2 makes a tasty, quickly prepared soup on its own. Serve with freshly made wholemeal toast and a wedge of sharp Farmhouse Cheddar or Stilton cheese.

WATCHPOINTS
Do not allow the onions to catch or they will give a bitter taste to the soup.
The standing time allows the bread to absorb the liquid and the crusts to soak, giving a better result to the finished bread and cheese soup.

●380 calories/1575 kj per portion

6 Place the bowls in a small roasting tin to catch any drips during cooking. Sprinkle the top of each bowl with 1 teaspoon Parmesan cheese. Bake above centre of oven for 15-20 minutes or until heated through and golden brown on top. Stand each bowl on an individual serving plate, then sprinkle soup with remaining Parmesan. Serve hot.

Speedy soup

SERVES 4

750 g/1½ lb potatoes, diced (see Buying guide)
1 tablespoon vegetable oil
1 large onion, finely chopped
600 ml/1 pint chicken stock
salt and freshly ground black pepper
200 g/7 oz can corned beef, diced
215 g/7½ oz can sweetcorn, drained
1 tablespoon chopped parsley

1 Heat the oil in a large saucepan, add the onion and cook gently for 2-3 minutes. Add the potatoes and cook for a further 1-2 minutes, stirring with a wooden spoon.
2 Stir the stock into the pan, season lightly with salt and pepper and bring to the boil. Lower the heat, cover and simmer for 10 minutes.
3 Add the corned beef and sweetcorn, bring back to the boil, then lower the heat again and simmer for a further 10 minutes.
4 Stir in parsley, taste and adjust seasoning, then pour into warmed soup bowls. Serve at once.

Quick beef and tomato consommé

SERVES 4-6

2 × 425 g/15 oz cans beef consomme
40 g/1½ oz margarine or butter
3 shallots, very finely chopped
300 ml/½ pint tomato juice
1 teaspoon caster sugar
1 tablespoon chopped parsley
1 small bay leaf
salt and freshly ground black pepper

1 Melt the margarine in a large saucepan. Add the shallots and fry gently until softened.
2 Stir in the consommé, tomato juice, sugar, parsley, bay leaf and salt and pepper to taste. Bring to the boil, then lower the heat and simmer gently for 15 minutes.
3 Discard the bay leaf. Taste and adjust seasoning, and serve hot.

Cheesy potato soup

SERVES 4

750 g/1½ lb potatoes, cut into even-sized pieces
salt
25 g/1 oz margarine or butter
1 large onion, finely chopped
2 large cloves garlic, finely chopped (optional)
3 celery stalks, finely chopped
1 large carrot, diced small
¼ small swede (weighing about 50 g/2 oz), diced small
300 ml/½ pint chicken or vegetable stock (see Cook's tip)
150 ml/¼ pint milk
½ teaspoon dried thyme or marjoram
½ teaspoon celery salt
freshly ground black pepper
75 g/3 oz Cheddar cheese, grated
3 tablespoons chopped parsley

1 Cook the potatoes in boiling salted water to cover for about 15 minutes or until tender.
2 When the potatoes are cooked, leave them to cool slightly in the water, then transfer both potatoes and water to a blender and blend until smooth. (If you do not have a blender, pass them through a sieve.) Return the purée to the rinsed-out pan.
3 Melt the margarine in a large frying-pan, add the onion and garlic, if using, and fry over moderate heat until beginning to soften. Add the remaining vegetables to the pan and cook, stirring occasionally, for about 10 minutes, until just beginning to colour.
4 Mix the vegetables with the potato purée in the saucepan, then stir in the stock, milk, thyme and celery salt. Add pepper to taste.
5 Bring to the boil, lower the heat and simmer gently for about 15 minutes or until the vegetables are just soft. ⚠ Stir in the cheese, reserving 2 tablespoons, and simmer for a further 2-3 minutes. Taste and adjust seasoning.
6 Pour into a warmed soup tureen. Sprinkle with the chopped parsley and the remaining cheese and serve at once.

Chilled courgette and cheese soup

SERVES 6

500 g/1 lb courgettes, cut into 2.5 cm/1 inch lengths
850 ml/1½ pints chicken stock
1 mint sprig
25 g/1 oz margarine or butter
1 onion, chopped
1 clove garlic, crushed (optional)
175 g/6 oz full-fat soft cheese (see Economy)
150 ml/¼ pint milk
salt and freshly ground black pepper

TO SERVE

6 ice cubes
2 tablespoons double cream (see Economy)
extra mint sprigs, to garnish

1 Put the courgettes into a large pan with the stock and mint sprig. Bring to the boil, then lower the heat and simmer for 10 minutes.
2 Meanwhile, melt the margarine in a small pan, add the onion and garlic, if using, and fry gently for 5 minutes until the onion is soft and lightly coloured.
3 Remove the courgettes from the heat and stir in the onion and garlic. Allow to cool slightly, then pour the courgette mixture into a blender and work to a purée.
4 In a large bowl, blend the cheese with the milk a little at a time, then beat with a wooden spoon until smooth and creamy. Stir in the courgette purée.
5 Pour the soup into a clean large bowl or soup tureen, cover and refrigerate for about 4 hours or overnight.
6 To serve: season the soup to taste with salt and pepper (see Cook's tip). Add ice cubes, swirl over the cream and sprinkle with sprigs of mint. Serve at once.

Cook's Notes

 TIME
15 minutes preparation, cooking time 10 minutes, then chilling for 4 hours or overnight.

 VARIATION
Instead of courgettes, use 1 large cucumber cut into 2 cm/¾ inch lengths.

 ECONOMY
For a less expensive soup lower in calories, use a curd cheese or Quark instead of full-fat cheese and natural yoghurt instead of the double cream.

 COOK'S TIP
Wait until the soup has chilled and the flavours have developed before adding the seasoning.

 SERVING IDEAS
Served just with fresh rolls or crusty bread and butter, this soup makes a delicious lunch for a hot day.

● 180 calories/750 kj per portion

Iced shrimp soup

SERVES 4

200 g/7 oz can shrimps in brine
2 tablespoons vegetable oil
1 onion, chopped
3 celery stalks, chopped
850 ml/1½ pints light fish, chicken
   or vegetable stock
2 tablespoons tomato purée
salt and freshly ground black pepper
150 ml/¼ pint single cream
snipped celery leaves, to garnish

1 Heat the oil in a saucepan. Add the onion and celery and cook for 2 minutes until onion is soft but not coloured. Add the stock and tomato purée and season to taste with salt and pepper. [!] Bring to the boil, stirring, then lower the heat, cover and simmer the stock for about 30 minutes, or until the vegetables are all quite tender.

2 Remove from the heat and leave to cool slightly, then pour into the goblet of a blender and work until smooth. Allow to cool completely, then refrigerate for about 4 hours, or overnight, until well chilled.

3 To serve: stir in the shrimps, including the brine, then stir in the cream until well incorporated. Taste and adjust the seasoning, if necessary. Ladle the soup into individual bowls and serve cold, garnished with the snipped celery leaves on top (see Special occasion).

Salami and tomato soup

SERVES 4

50 g/2 oz sliced salami, skinned and
   roughly chopped
15 g/½ oz butter
100 g/4 oz potatoes, diced
100 g/4 oz carrots, diced
1 onion, roughly chopped
1 teaspoon sweet paprika
225 g/8 oz can chopped tomatoes
150 ml/¼ pint tomato juice
425 ml/¾ pint chicken stock
¼ teaspoon dried rosemary
salt and freshly ground white pepper
400 g/14 oz can cannellini beans,
   drained
1 tablespoon chopped fresh parsley

SESAME CROUTONS

25 g/1 oz butter, softened
1 tablespoon sesame seeds
1 teaspoon French mustard
4 thick slices white bread, crusts
   removed

1 Melt the butter in a saucepan, add
the potatoes, carrots, onion and
paprika and cook gently for 5
minutes until the onions are soft.

2 Stir in the tomatoes and their
liquid, the tomato juice and stock
then bring to the boil. Lower the
heat, stir in the rosemary and season
with salt and pepper. Cover and
simmer for 20 minutes until the
vegetables are tender.

3 Remove from the heat and leave to
cool slightly, then purée in a blender
or work through a sieve.

4 Make the croûtons: put the butter
in a bowl and beat in the sesame
seeds and mustard. Spread on one
side of each slice of bread. Cut the

bread into 2 cm/¾ inch cubes and
put them in a frying-pan. Cook
gently for 5 minutes or until they are
golden, turning frequently.

5 Return the soup to the rinsed-out
pan and stir in the salami. Add
the beans and heat through gently
for 5 minutes, then taste and adjust
the seasoning if necessary.

6 Ladle the soup into warmed
individual bowls or a soup tureen,
top with the sesame croûtons and
then sprinkle over the chopped
parsley. Serve the soup at once.

Cook's Notes

 TIME
Preparation takes 20
minutes and cooking
about 25 minutes.

VARIATIONS
Use ham or garlic
sausage instead of the
salami. Red kidney beans or
butter beans could be used
instead of cannellini beans.

 ECONOMY
Use any left-over
cooked meat such as
pork or chicken for this recipe.

FOR CHILDREN
Use sliced frankfurters
or cooked pork sausages
instead of the salami.

FREEZING
Cool completely, then
transfer to a rigid con-
tainer. Seal, label and freeze for
up to 3 months. To serve: reheat
from frozen, then stir in the
beans and cook for a further 5
minutes while making the
sesame croûtons.

● 330 calories/1375 kj per portion

Pea soup with cheese toast

SERVES 4

540 g/1 lb 3 oz can garden peas
1 tablespoon dried onion flakes
2 tablespoons boiling water
300 ml/½ pint chicken stock
½ teaspoon dried thyme
3 tablespoons instant potato powder (see Cook's tip)
1-2 teaspoons lemon juice
2-3 tablespoons evaporated milk or single cream
salt and freshly ground black pepper
1 tablespoon finely chopped fresh parsley

TOAST

4 small thick slices wholemeal bread
50 g/2 oz Cheddar cheese, grated
2 tablespoons evaporated milk or single cream
¼ teaspoon made English mustard

1 Put the dried onion flakes into a cup, pour over the boiling water and leave to stand for at least 15 minutes.
2 Put the peas with their liquid in the goblet of a liquidizer with the onion mixture and blend until smooth. Work through a sieve. Put into a saucepan with the stock and thyme and bring to the boil over moderate heat.
3 Lower the heat and sprinkle in the potato powder. Stir for 1-2 minutes then remove from heat and stir in the lemon juice and milk. Season to taste with salt and pepper. Return to the heat and simmer gently while you prepare the toast.
4 Heat the grill to high, and toast the bread on both sides. Remove from the grill.
5 Mix the cheese with the milk, mustard and salt and pepper.
6 Spread the cheese mixture on the toast, return to the grill and grill until the cheese mixture browns.
7 Ladle the soup into warmed individual bowls. Cut each slice of toast into 4 and serve at once.

Cook's Notes

 TIME Preparation and cooking, including the time needed for soaking the dried onion, is about 40 minutes.

 VARIATIONS Instead of dried onion flakes, add some onion salt to the soup or use dried mint instead of thyme. For a more substantial soup, top with grated Cheddar cheese and chopped parsley.

COOK'S TIP Instant potato powder thickens the soup and gives it a good texture. Use potato flour or cornflour instead, if wished, but they must be worked to a paste with a little cold water first.

●270 calories/1135 kj per portion

Spinach and liver pâté soup

SERVES 4

850 g/1 lb 12 oz can cream of
    chicken soup
225 g/8 oz chopped frozen spinach,
    defrosted, or canned spinach,
    drained
100 g/4 oz liver pâté (see Buying
    guide)
a little milk (optional)
2 teaspoons lemon juice
salt and freshly ground black pepper

TO GARNISH

25 g/1 oz margarine or butter
4 streaky bacon rashers, rinds
    removed and chopped
2 slices white bread, crusts removed
    and cut into small dice

1 Heat the oven to 110C/225F/
Gas ¼. Make the garnish: melt the
margarine in a frying-pan. Add the
bacon and fry briskly for 2-3
minutes to release any fat. Add the
diced bread and fry over moderate
to high heat until both bacon and
bread are lightly browned and crisp.
Drain the bacon and croûtons well
on absorbent paper and keep hot in
the oven.
2 Pour the soup into a large saucepan, add the spinach and heat
gently until simmering.
3 Using a balloon whisk, gradually
whisk the liver pâté into the soup. If
the soup seems too thick, add a little
milk. Add the lemon juice and
season carefully with salt and
pepper.
4 Serve the soup piping hot in
warmed individual soup bowls,
sprinkled with the crispy bacon
pieces and the croûtons.

Celery and peanut soup

SERVES 4

4 large celery stalks, chopped (see Economy)

6 tablespoons crunchy peanut butter

15 g/½ oz margarine or butter
1 tablespoon vegetable oil
1 onion, chopped
700 ml/1¼ pints light stock
salt and freshly ground black pepper
4 tablespoons single cream, to serve
chopped celery leaves, to garnish

1 Heat the margarine and oil in a saucepan, add the celery and onion and fry gently for 5 minutes until the onion is soft and lightly coloured.
2 Add the stock and bring to the boil. Lower the heat, cover and simmer gently for about 30 minutes until the celery is tender.
3 Cool the mixture a little, then work in a blender for a few seconds until smooth.
4 Return to the rinsed-out pan, place over low heat, then whisk in the peanut butter. Heat through until just boiling. ✳ Taste and then adjust seasoning.
5 Ladle the soup into 4 warmed individual bowls. Stir 1 tablespoon cream into each, then wait for a few seconds for the cream to rise to the surface. Sprinkle the chopped celery leaves in the centre of the bowls and serve at once.

Cook's Notes

TIME
Total preparation and cooking time is about 45 minutes.

FREEZING
Cool quickly, then pour into a rigid container, leaving 2 cm/¾ inch headspace. Seal, label and freeze for up to 2 months. To serve: defrost at room temperature for 2 hours, then reheat in a heavy-based pan, stirring frequently until bubbling. Taste and adjust seasoning, then proceed from the beginning of stage 5.

ECONOMY
This is a good way of using up outside celery stalks which may be a little tough, saving the more tender inner stalks for use in salads or serving with cheese.

SERVING IDEAS
Serve with freshly baked bread or rolls— crunchy brown granary rolls or those coated with a sprinkling of sesame or poppy seeds go particularly well with this soup.

● 265 calories/1100 kj per portion

Hot melon soup

SERVES 4-6

3 × 300 g/10 oz cans condensed
   chicken soup (see Buying guide)

1 cantaloupe or honeydew melon,
   quartered, peeled and deseeded
   (see Buying guide)
1 teaspoon sugar
½ teaspoon salt
100 g/4 oz pork tenderloin, sliced
   into fine strips
2 teaspoons light soy sauce
sliced button mushrooms, to garnish

1 Put the chicken soup in a large
saucepan and make up with water
according to label instructions.
Bring gently to the boil.
2 Meanwhile, chop the melon flesh
roughly into 1 cm/½ inch dice,
reserving as much of its juice as
possible in a bowl.
3 When the soup is boiling, add the
diced melon and its juice, the sugar
and salt. Bring the soup back to

 Cook's Notes

TIME
Preparation takes no
more than 10 minutes
and cooking 7-8 minutes.

BUYING GUIDE
If plain chicken soup is
not available, cans of
condensed chicken noodle soup
or condensed chicken and rice
soup give equally good results.
Alternatively, use 600 ml/
1 pint homemade chicken stock.
   Buy unblemished ripe melons
with a strong fragrance and
which yield slightly in the palm
of the hand.

VARIATIONS
For a lighter dish, try
substituting 100 g/4 oz

sliced button mushrooms for
the pork tenderloin.
   For a pronounced oriental
flavour, put a thin slice of fresh
ginger root in soup at stage 1
and remove before serving.

 WATCHPOINTS
This dish has a quite
distinctive and subtle
flavour; it is easily lost with
even slight over-seasoning.
   Use exactly the amount of salt
suggested in recipe and no
more than the suggested
amount of soy sauce. Do not
use any pepper, but pass
freshly ground black pepper
separately, if wished.

●285 calories/1175 kj per portion

the boil and simmer it gently for
5 minutes only.
4 Add the shredded pork to the
pan. Bring back to the boil and
simmer for another 2-3 minutes.

Add the soy sauce then pour into
warmed individual soup bowls.
Serve the hot melon soup at once,
garnished with the sliced button
mushrooms.

Oxtail dumpling soup

SERVES 4

600 ml/1 pint packet oxtail soup powder (see Variations)
600 ml/1 pint cold water
100 g/4 oz carrot, coarsely grated
100 g/4 oz swede, coarsely grated

DUMPLINGS

100 g/4 oz self-raising flour
40 g/1½ oz shredded suet
½ teaspoon mustard powder
¼ teaspoon dried mixed herbs
100 g/4 oz corned beef, finely chopped
salt and freshly ground black pepper
about 4 tablespoons water

1 Make the dumplings: sift the flour into a bowl and add the suet, mustard, herbs and corned beef. Season with salt and pepper, then make a well in the centre and add a little water. Gradually work the dry ingredients into the centre until evenly mixed, adding just enough water to form a fairly firm dough. Divide into 12 portions then roll each into a ball.

2 Put the soup powder into a wide pan, add the water and bring to the boil, stirring occasionally.

3 Add the carrot and swede then, when the soup is just coming back to the boil, drop the dumplings into it. Lower the heat and simmer, covered, for 18-20 minutes, stirring occasionally to prevent sticking.

4 Spoon into individual warmed bowls and serve at once.

Mulligatawny pot

SERVES 4

425 g/15 oz can mulligatawny soup
25 g/1 oz margarine or butter
 1 onion, chopped
250 g/9 oz potatoes, cut into 1 cm/
   ½ inch cubes
salt
 2 large eggs, hard-boiled and
   chopped (see Preparation)
freshly ground black pepper
4-6 poppadoms, to serve (optional,
   see Buying guide)
vegetable oil, for frying (optional)
2 tablespoons chopped parsley

1 Melt the margarine in a large saucepan, add the onion and cook gently for about 5 minutes until soft but not brown.
2 Put the potatoes into a saucepan, cover with cold water, add salt, cover and boil for 5 minutes or until the potatoes are just tender. ⚠ Drain thoroughly.
3 Without breaking them up, carefully mix the potatoes with the softened onion, raise the heat and

continue to cook, stirring, until the potatoes are lightly browned.
4 Add the soup to the pan and bring just to the boil. Mix in the chopped eggs and season lightly with salt and pepper. Heat through and keep hot.

5 Fry the poppadoms, if using, in hot oil, or grill them.
6 Pour the mulligatawny into warmed individual soup plates and sprinkle with parsley. If serving poppadoms hand them separately.

Mexican chilli soup

SERVES 4

175 g/6 oz lean minced beef
1 tablespoon corn oil
1 large onion, chopped
½ teaspoon ground cumin
15 g/½ oz plain flour
225 g/8 oz can tomatoes
½ teaspoon Tabasco (see
   Variations)
850 ml/1½ pints beef stock
salt and freshly ground black pepper
425 g/15 oz can red kidney beans,
   drained (see Variations)
fresh coriander or flat-leaved
   parsley, to garnish (optional)

1 Heat the oil in a saucepan and
add the onion, minced beef and
cumin. Cook over high heat until
the meat is evenly browned, stirring

with a wooden spoon to remove any lumps and mix thoroughly.
2 Sprinkle in the flour and stir well, then add the tomatoes with their juice, the Tabasco and the stock.
3 Bring to the boil, stirring. Season to taste with salt and pepper and

simmer, uncovered, for 25 minutes.
4 Add the drained beans, stir them in and cook for a further 5 minutes or until heated through. Transfer to a warmed serving dish, sprinkle with coriander, if liked, then serve the soup at once (see Serving ideas).

Country soup

SERVES 4

1 potato, diced
1 large onion, sliced
1 small head celery, sliced
¼ head firm cabbage, shredded
225 g/8 oz can tomatoes
850 ml/1½ pints beef or ham
   stock
225 g/8 oz can kidney beans,
   drained
1 large or 2 medium frankfurter
   sausages
50 g/2 oz garlic sausage or salami,
   diced
50 g/2 oz smoked sausage, diced
salt and freshly ground black pepper
1 tablespoon finely chopped
   fresh parsley

1 Put the potato, onion, celery and cabbage in a large saucepan. Add the tomatoes with their juice, breaking them up against the sides of the pan with a wooden spoon.

2 Add the stock to the pan and bring quickly to the boil. Lower the heat to moderate, cover and simmer for 40 minutes.

3 Add the kidney beans, cover and cook for a further 20 minutes.

4 Meanwhile, bring a pan of water to the boil. Put the frankfurters into it and heat them through for 2 minutes. Remove with a slotted spoon and slice.

5 Add the garlic and smoked sausage and the frankfurters to the soup. Simmer over low heat for 15 minutes. Taste and adjust seasoning, [!] then pour into warmed individual soup bowls and sprinkle with chopped parsley. Serve at once.

Cook's Notes

TIME
Preparation takes about 20 minutes and cooking about 1¼ hours.

WATCHPOINT
The sausages can make the soup quite salty so do not add any extra salt until you have tasted it. If using ham stock, you will not need to use any salt at all.

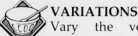

VARIATIONS
Vary the vegetables in this soup according to what is in season and what is available. Leeks and carrots make tasty additions.

●265 calories/1125 kj per portion

Carrot soup with egg and rice

SERVES 4-8

750 g/1½ lb new carrots, thinly
    sliced
25 g/1 oz margarine or butter
600 ml/1 pint chicken stock
1 teaspoon sugar
salt and freshly ground black pepper
150 ml/¼ pint milk
75 g/3 oz cooked rice (see Cook's
    tips)
4 eggs at room temperature (see
    Cook's tips)
2 spring onions, finely chopped
150 ml/¼ pint single cream

1 Melt the margarine in a saucepan, add the carrots and fry gently for 2-3 minutes to soften slightly.
2 Add the chicken stock and sugar and season to taste with salt and pepper. Bring to the boil, then lower the heat and simmer, uncovered, for 30 minutes or until the carrots are very tender.
3 Remove the pan from the heat and allow mixture to cool slightly, then pour it into the goblet of a blender and work for a few seconds until smooth. Return the purée to the rinsed-out pan and stir in the milk and the cooked rice. Taste and adjust the seasoning, if necessary.
4 Heat the soup gently until hot but not boiling, then break in the eggs and poach them for about 8 minutes or until they are firm enough to be lifted out with a slotted spoon.
5 Spoon an egg into each of 4 warmed soup bowls and pour over the soup. Sprinkle over the spring onions, swirl in the cream and serve the soup at once.

Cook's Notes

TIME
Preparation takes 15 minutes, cooking takes about 50 minutes.

SERVING IDEAS
This is a fairly substantial soup, so serve with a light accompaniment such as Melba toast or a selection of crispbreads.

COOK'S TIPS
If cooking raw rice for this dish, you will need 25 g/1 oz to provide 75 g/3 oz of cooked rice.
Remove the eggs from the refrigerator 1 hour before using: cold eggs will require a longer time to set.

●155 calories/650 kj per portion

Suppers

Over 30 of the suppers chosen
are non-meat dishes, including crunchy salads,
fresh vegetable dishes, omelettes, flans and quiches.
There are also plenty of budget-conscious fish and
meat recipes for family cooking.

Barley and bacon hotpot

SERVES 4
250 g/9 oz pearl barley
25 g/1 oz margarine or butter
250 g/9 oz streaky bacon, rinds
   removed and finely chopped
2 large onions, thinly sliced
250 g/9 oz carrots, thinly sliced
175 g/6 oz celery, chopped
100 g/4 oz mushrooms, thinly sliced
600 ml/1 pint chicken stock
4 tablespoons chopped fresh
   parsley
salt and freshly ground black pepper

1 Heat the oven to 180C/350F/Gas 4.
2 Melt the margarine in a flameproof casserole. Add the bacon and onions and fry gently for 5 minutes until the onions are soft and lightly coloured.
3 Stir in the carrots, celery, mushrooms and pearl barley, then pour in the stock and bring to the boil. Add the parsley and salt and pepper to taste.

4 Cover the casserole and cook in the oven for 1 hour, or until the barley is soft and nearly all the liquid absorbed. Serve hot.

Aubergine and bacon savoury

SERVES 4

500 g/1 lb aubergines, cut into 5 mm/¼ inch slices
salt
2 tablespoons olive oil (see Economy)
250 g/9 oz rashers streaky bacon, rinds removed and diced
50 g/2 oz Parmesan cheese, grated (see Economy)
150 ml/¼ pint milk
freshly ground black pepper
2 tablespoons chopped parsley, to garnish
margarine, for greasing

1 Put the aubergine slices in a single layer on a board or work surface and sprinkle evenly with 1 tablespoon salt. Leave to stand 30 minutes to remove the bitter juices.
2 Heat the oven to 190C/375F/Gas 5 and grease an ovenproof dish.
3 Rinse the aubergine slices under cold running water, pat dry with absorbent paper and set aside.
4 Heat the oil in a large frying-pan, add the aubergine slices and fry over moderate heat, turning once, until golden on both sides. Drain on absorbent paper.
5 Put the bacon in the frying-pan and fry it gently until lightly browned. Drain on absorbent paper.
6 Arrange a layer of aubergines in the base of the prepared dish, then a layer of bacon and a layer of cheese. Repeat twice, so that you have 3 layers of each. Season the milk well with salt and pepper and pour it over the top.
7 Bake in the oven for 35-40 minutes, until the top is golden.
8 Serve hot, sprinkled with the chopped parsley.

Lamb and pasta medley

SERVES 4

500 g/1 lb minced raw lamb
2 tablespoons olive oil
1 onion, chopped
1 green pepper, deseeded and chopped
2 courgettes, finely chopped
400 g/14 oz can tomatoes
300 ml/½ pint water
250 g/9 oz pasta shapes
½ teaspoon dried basil
½ teaspoon dried thyme
salt and freshly ground black pepper
100 g/4 oz mushrooms, sliced

1 Heat the oil in a saucepan and fry the onion, green pepper and courgettes gently for 2-3 minutes until they are beginning to soften.

2 Add the lamb, turn the heat to high and fry until the meat is evenly browned, stirring with a wooden spoon to remove any lumps. Pour off any excess fat.

3 Stir in the tomatoes with their juice and the water, breaking up the tomatoes with the spoon. Bring to the boil, stirring frequently.

4 Add the pasta, herbs and salt and pepper to taste and mix well. Cover the pan and simmer the lamb and pasta for 15 minutes.

5 Stir in mushrooms and simmer, uncovered, for 10 minutes. Serve the lamb and pasta medley at once (see Serving ideas and Variations).

Cook's Notes

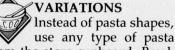
TIME
About 45 minutes to prepare and cook.

VARIATIONS
Instead of pasta shapes, use any type of pasta from the store cupboard. Break up spaghetti into small pieces.

Minced beef can be used as an alternative to the lamb.

Dried mixed herbs may be used instead of the dried basil and thyme.

SERVING IDEAS
This dish needs no accompaniment as it is a meal in itself, but grated hard cheese such as Parmesan or mature Cheddar may be served separately for sprinkling.

ECONOMY
Use left-over cooked lamb, chopped finely, and omit all of stage 2.

●570 calories/2375 kj per portion

Spiced smoked haddie

 SERVES 4
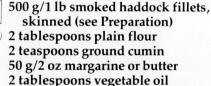
500 g/1 lb smoked haddock fillets,
    skinned (see Preparation)
2 tablespoons plain flour
2 teaspoons ground cumin
50 g/2 oz margarine or butter
2 tablespoons vegetable oil

SAUCE
150 g/5 oz natural yoghurt
½ small cucumber, cut into 5 mm/
    ¼ inch dice
2 spring onions, finely chopped
salt and freshly ground black pepper

1 First make the sauce: put the
yoghurt, cucumber and spring
onions into a bowl. Season with salt

and pepper to taste and stir well to
mix. Transfer the sauce to a small
bowl and set aside in a cool place or
in the refrigerator, while the fish is
cooking.
2 Cut each haddock fillet into strips
1 cm/½ inch wide. Put the flour and
cumin into a polythene bag. Add
the haddock and shake the bag until
the fish is evenly coated in flour.
Shake off any excess.
3 Heat the margarine with the oil in
a wide non-stick frying-pan then
add the haddock strips and fry for
4-5 minutes, turning them several
times until they are evenly brown
on all sides.
4 Remove the fish from the pan
with a fish slice, quickly spread
them out on absorbent paper to
drain, then transfer them to a heated
serving dish. Serve at once, with the
bowl of yoghurt sauce handed
separately.

Cook's Notes

 TIME
Total preparation and
cooking time is 40
minutes.

 SERVING IDEAS
Serve with broad or
runner beans and brown
rice or new potatoes boiled in
their skins.

 PREPARATION
To skin the fillets: place
the fish on a board, skin
side down and, using a sharp
knife, loosen the skin at the
narrow end then push the flesh
away from the skin along the
fillet.

●220 calories/925 kj per portion

52

Layered fish pancakes

SERVES 4

175 g/6 oz plain flour
pinch of salt
2 eggs, beaten
425 ml/¾ pint milk
butter or vegetable oil, for frying
and greasing

FILLING

850 ml/1½ pints milk
2 slices onion
1 bay leaf
10 black peppercorns
750 g/1½ lb haddock fillets
(smoked or fresh)
40 g/1½ oz margarine or butter
40 g/1½ oz plain flour
salt and freshly ground black pepper
½ teaspoon sweet paprika

1 Make the pancakes: sift the flour and salt into a bowl, then make a well in the centre. Add the eggs and a little of the milk and whisk together slowly. Pour in the remaining milk and whisk to a smooth batter.

2 Heat a little butter or oil in a heavy-based 18 cm/7 inch frying-pan over moderate to high heat. Pour off any excess.

3 Remove the pan from the heat and pour about 1½ tablespoons batter into the pan. Return the pan to the heat and cook until the batter is set on the underside. Turn over and lightly cook the other side, then lift on to a sheet of greaseproof paper.

4 Continue making pancakes in this way, interleaving each with greaseproof paper until you have used all the batter. You should have 10 pancakes.

5 Heat the oven to 180C/350F/Gas 4.

6 Make the fish sauce: put the milk into a large shallow pan with the onion slices, bay leaf and peppercorns. Add the fish fillets, bring the milk to the boil, then lower the heat and simmer for 10 minutes.

7 Lift the fish out of the pan with a slotted spoon and set aside until cool enough to handle.

8 Strain the fish cooking liquid into a measuring jug, measure 600 ml/1 pint and reserve. Melt the margarine in a clean saucepan, sprinkle in the flour and stir over low heat for 1-2 minutes until straw-coloured. Remove from the heat and gradually stir in the measured liquid. Return to the heat and simmer, stirring, until thick and smooth. Set aside.

9 Flake the cooked fish, discarding any skin and bones.

10 Pour off 150 ml/¼ pint of the sauce from the pan and reserve. Add the fish to the sauce remaining in the pan, folding it in gently. Add salt and pepper to taste.

11 Brush a shallow ovenproof dish lightly with butter or oil. Put a pancake on the bottom of the dish, then spread with a little of the mixture. Cover with another pancake, then continue to layer pancakes and sauce in this way until all the ingredients are used.

12 Spoon the reserved 150 ml/¼ pint sauce over the top of the pancakes and sprinkle with paprika. Bake in the oven for 25 minutes. Serve hot, straight from the dish.

Cook's Notes

TIME
Preparation and pre-cooking take 1 hour. Baking in the oven takes 25 minutes.

VARIATION
Use any sort of white or smoked fish or a mixture of two or more varieties.

SERVING IDEAS
Garnish with 50 g/2 oz peeled prawns or with tomato slices.

●625 calories/2625 kj per pancake

Quick beef curry

SERVES 4

500 g/1 lb lean minced beef
1 large onion, chopped

1 clove garlic, crushed (optional)
1 tablespoon curry powder (see Did you know)
¼ teaspoon ground ginger
¼ teaspoon ground cumin
1 dessert apple, peeled and grated
2 tablespoons sultanas or seedless raisins
300 g/10 oz can condensed beef consommé
salt and freshly ground black pepper
100 g/4 oz mushrooms, quartered

Cook's Notes

TIME
A quick and easy dish taking about 40 minutes to prepare and cook.

DID YOU KNOW
Curry powder is made from many different spices, including allspice, cardamom, chilli, cumin, saffron and turmeric. It is available in various strengths, from mild to very hot, so be sure to check the label carefully.

SERVING IDEAS
Serve with boiled rice and sliced onions.

●400 calories/1675 kj per portion

1 Place the beef, onion and garlic in a saucepan and fry over moderate heat until the beef is well browned, stirring constantly to break up lumps.
2 Stir in the spices and cook for 2 minutes, then stir in the apple, sultanas and the beef consommé. Season to taste with salt and pepper.
3 Bring to the boil, then simmer gently for 5 minutes.
4 Stir in the mushrooms and simmer a further 10 minutes. Taste and adjust seasoning. Serve at once.

Oriental steak salad

SERVES 4

175 g/6 oz rump steak (see Buying
    guide)
salt
100 g/4 oz long-grain rice
100 g/4 oz frozen peas
1 large carrot, grated
1 teaspoon ground ginger
freshly ground black pepper
150 g/5 oz beansprouts
50 g/2 oz button mushrooms, sliced

MARINADE

50 ml/2 fl oz red wine
2 tablespoons soy sauce
1 tablespoon lemon juice
2.5 cm/1 inch piece root ginger,
    peeled and grated (see Buying
    guide)
2 teaspoons dark soft brown sugar

TO GARNISH

lettuce leaves
25 g/1 oz flaked almonds
cucumber slices

1 Bring a pan of salted water to the boil and cook the long-grain rice for about 12 minutes until just tender. Drain and rinse under cold running water for 1 minute. Drain again.

2 Cook the peas according to packet directions then drain and rinse under cold water. Mix the rice, peas and grated carrot together in a bowl. Cover and refrigerate.

3 Heat the grill to very hot. Rub the ground ginger evenly over both sides of the steak together with salt and pepper to taste. Grill for 5-7 minutes on either side then leave the steak to cool slightly.

4 Mix the marinade ingredients in a jug with ½ teaspoon salt.

5 Slice the steak into very thin strips then put in a bowl and pour over the marinade. Stir the meat to make sure it is thoroughly coated, then leave in a cool place for 3-4 hours, stirring occasionally.

6 When ready to serve, remove the steak with a slotted spoon and reserve the marinade. Stir the meat, the beansprouts and the mushrooms into the rice mixture. Then add 2 tablespoons of the marinade and gently mix it in.

7 To serve: arrange the lettuce leaves in a salad bowl, pile the salad in the centre then sprinkle over the almonds and garnish with cucumber slices.

Cook's Notes

TIME
The salad takes about 20 minutes to prepare but the steak should marinate for 3-4 hours after it has been cooked.

SERVING IDEAS
This makes a tasty supper on its own.

BUYING GUIDE
Although rump steak is expensive, very little is needed for this dish.

If root ginger is hard to find, mix 1 teaspoon of ground ginger into the marinade instead.

●260 calories/1075 kj per portion

Chicken biriani

SERVES 4-6

350 g/12 oz cooked chicken, cut into cubes
50 g/2 oz butter
225 g/8 oz long-grain rice
2 tablespoons Madras curry powder
50 g/2 oz seedless raisins
16 black peppercorns
¼ teaspoon salt
1 chicken stock cube
850 ml/1½ pints hot water
1 large onion, quartered
25 g/1 oz flaked almonds
1 hard-boiled egg, quartered lengthways, to garnish

1 Melt 25 g/1 oz butter in a heavy-based saucepan and fry the rice over moderate heat for about 1 minute, until the rice is only just beginning to brown on all sides.

2 Lower the heat, add half the curry powder and stir well. Reserve a few raisins and add the rest to the pan with the peppercorns and salt.
3 Crumble the stock cube into the water, stir to dissolve and add to the rice mixture. Cover the pan and cook gently for about 10 minutes until the rice is almost cooked but there is still some liquid left in the bottom of the pan.
5 Meanwhile, melt the remaining butter in a frying-pan and add the chicken and onion. Fry gently for

about 2 minutes, turning the chicken and onion frequently.
6 Add the remaining curry powder and fry quickly, stirring well, until the chicken is brown and well coated in spices while the onion stays crisp.
7 Add the chicken mixture to the rice. Reserve a few almonds and stir into the pan. Cook gently until all the remaining liquid is absorbed. Serve at once, garnished with the reserved raisins and almonds and the hard-boiled egg quarters.

Cook's Notes

 TIME
This tasty dish takes only about 25 minutes to prepare and cook.

SERVING IDEAS
Serve accompanied by mango chutney and a side dish of natural yoghurt mixed with chopped fresh mint.

? DID YOU KNOW
Birianis are normally finished by drizzling saffron water or food colouring over them so that some of the grains of rice turn a golden yellow to contrast vividly with those that remain white.

●520 calories/2175 kj per portion

Cheesy burgers

SERVES 4

**750 g/1½ lb chuck steak, trimmed
    and minced (see Buying guide)**
1 onion, finely chopped
freshly ground black pepper
½ teaspoon celery salt (optional)
100 g/4 oz Stilton cheese
1 teaspoon French mustard
1 tablespoon Worcestershire sauce
1 tablespoon top of the milk
2 tablespoons vegetable oil
**8 streaky bacon rashers, cut into 3 or
    4 pieces**
sweet paprika (optional)
**shredded lettuce and tomato
    wedges, to garnish**

1 Mix the minced steak with the chopped onion and season to taste with pepper and celery salt, if using. Divide the mixture into 8 portions and form into even-sized burgers. Refrigerate until ready to cook.
2 In a bowl, mash the Stilton cheese with a fork. Work in the mustard, Worcestershire sauce and top of the milk, to blend thoroughly.
3 Heat the grill to moderate. Heat the oven to 110C/225F/Gas ¼.
4 Heat the oil in a large frying-pan until very hot. Add the burgers and fry over high heat for about 2 minutes on either side. Turn down the heat and fry for a further 5 minutes on each side.
5 While the burgers are cooking, grill the bacon pieces, turning them once. Keep them warm in the oven

and then turn the grill up to high.
6 Remove the burgers from the frying-pan with a slotted spoon and place on the grill pan. Spread them with the cheese mixture, dividing it equally between them. Put the burgers under the hot grill until the cheese is melted and bubbling and beginning to brown.
7 Sprinkle the burgers with a little sweet paprika, if liked, and top each one with some bacon pieces. Serve at once with lettuce and tomatoes.

Cook's Notes

TIME
Preparing the burgers and cheese topping takes about 20 minutes. Cooking the burgers takes about 15 minutes.

BUYING GUIDE
Chuck steak, providing all the fat is removed, makes very good hamburgers –better than butcher's mince. If you do not have a mincer, ask the butcher to do it for you.

FREEZING
Prepare the hamburgers as in stage 1. Open freeze without the cheesy topping until solid, then pack together in a freezer bag and freeze for up to 3 months. To serve: cook from frozen, allowing a few minutes longer frying time in stage 4. Prepare the cheese mixture as described in the recipe.

●600 calories/2525 kj per portion

Greek lamb roll

SERVES 4
215 g/7½ oz frozen puff pastry,
  defrosted
beaten egg, to glaze

FILLING
250 g/9 oz minced lamb (see Buying
  guide and Economy)
1 aubergine, weighing about
  250 g/9 oz, finely chopped
  (see Cook's tip)
1 clove garlic, crushed (optional)
25 g /1 oz fresh white breadcrumbs
1 egg, beaten
½ teaspoon dried oregano or
  mixed herbs
1 teaspoon chopped fresh mint
about ¼ teaspoon freshly grated
  nutmeg
50 g/2 oz Feta cheese, crumbled
salt and freshly ground black pepper

1 Heat the oven to 200C/400F/Gas 6.
2 Make the filling: in a bowl, mix
together all the ingredients for the
filling except the cheese. Season
with salt and pepper to taste.
3 Roll pastry on a floured surface

Cook's Notes

TIME
Preparation takes about
20 minutes and cooking
takes 35-40 minutes.

BUYING GUIDE
Minced lamb is usually
sold in supermarkets.
Otherwise, ask your butcher to
mince lamb for you as most
butchers will supply it only on
request. Minced beef can be
used as an alternative if lamb
is difficult to obtain.

ECONOMY
This is an excellent way
to use up left-over roast

lamb. Finely chop and mix with
the other filling ingredients. Because the aubergine needs long
cooking the roll still needs 35-40
minutes in the oven.

COOK'S TIP
The flavour of the dish
is best if the aubergine
is not peeled. For a less chewy
texture, blanch the aubergine
for 5 minutes before chopping it.

SERVING IDEAS
Serve the roll with
gravy or a tomato sauce.

●450 calories/1875 kj per portion

to make a 33 × 18 cm/13 × 7 inch
rectangle. Reserve trimmings.
4 Spoon half lamb mixture down
centre of the pastry to within
2.5 cm/1 inch of the 2 short ends.
Sprinkle the cheese on top and
cover with remaining lamb mixture.
Brush the edges of the pastry with
water. Seal the 2 long edges down
the length of the loaf, then tuck in
short ends and seal.
6 Dampen a baking sheet and place

roll, sealed side down, on it. Brush
with egg and cut 2 slashes on top.
7 Make decorations from the trimmings, brush undersides with
water and arrange on the loaf.
Brush all over with beaten egg.
Bake in the oven for 35-40 minutes
until filling is cooked through and
pastry is golden, covering the top
with foil or greaseproof paper if
it begins to overbrown. Transfer to
a serving plate and serve hot or cold.

Spiced whitebait

SERVES 4
750 g/1½ lb whitebait, defrosted if frozen
6 tablespoons plain flour
1 tablespoon sweet paprika
1 tablespoon ground cumin
2-2½ teaspoons chilli powder
1½ teaspoons ground coriander
1½ teaspoons salt
vegetable oil, for deep frying
lemon or lime wedges, to garnish

1 Heat the oven to 110C/225F/Gas ¼.
2 Pat the whitebait dry with absorbent paper. Mix the flour with the spices and salt in a bowl. Put one-third of the whitebait in a large polythene bag with 3 tablespoons of the flour mixture. Shake until the whitebait are evenly coated, transfer whitebait to a plate and repeat with the remaining flour and fish.
3 Meanwhile, heat the oil in a deep-fat frier to 190C/375F, or until a stale bread cube browns in 50 seconds.
4 Using a slotted spoon, lower a spoonful of whitebait into the hot oil. Cook for 2-3 minutes until lightly browned. Remove the fish with the slotted spoon then drain well on absorbent paper. Transfer to a serving plate and keep warm in the oven while frying the remaining fish. Check the temperature of the oil before adding each batch.
5 When all the fish are cooked, garnish with lemon wedges.

Cook's Notes

TIME
Preparation and cooking the whitebait take about 40 minutes.

SERVING IDEAS
Serve with thinly sliced buttered brown bread and a refreshing cucumber sambal: dice a small cucumber, put it in a bowl and mix in enough natural yoghurt to coat. Add salt, paprika and lemon juice to taste. Refrigerate until needed.
Chilled lager goes very well with this spicy fish dish.

● 765 calories/3200 kj per portion

Oatmeal and caraway chops

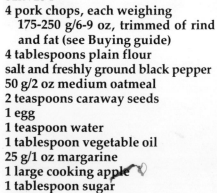

SERVES 4

4 pork chops, each weighing
175-250 g/6-9 oz, trimmed of rind
and fat (see Buying guide)
4 tablespoons plain flour
salt and freshly ground black pepper
50 g/2 oz medium oatmeal
2 teaspoons caraway seeds
1 egg
1 teaspoon water
1 tablespoon vegetable oil
25 g/1 oz margarine
1 large cooking apple
1 tablespoon sugar
parsley sprigs, to garnish

1 Spread the flour out on a flat plate
and season with salt and pepper.
Mix the oatmeal and caraway seeds
together on a separate flat plate and
season with salt and pepper. Beat
the egg in a shallow dish with the
teaspoon of water.

 TIME
Preparation and cook-
ing the pork chops
take about 35 minutes.

 BUYING GUIDE
Choose loin pork chops
or spare ribs. Pork fillet
can be used cut in thick slices –
1 slice per portion. It is more
expensive but needs less time to
cook than chops.

 SERVING IDEAS
Serve chops and apple
with cooked rice mixed
with lightly fried onion.

 WATCHPOINT
Keep the heat at mode-
rate so that the pork
chops cook thoroughly without
overbrowning the oatmeal.

●450 calories/1900 kj per portion

2 Dip the chops into the flour, then
into the beaten egg and then into
the oatmeal mixture, making sure
they are evenly coated.
3 Heat the oil and margarine in a
frying-pan, add the chops and fry
for 1 minute on each side over high
heat. Lower the heat to moderate
and continue cooking for 15 minutes, or until the chops are tender,
turning them once. !
4 Meanwhile, quarter the apple,
peel and core it, then cut the quar-

ters into thick wedges. Put the
sugar into a shallow dish and dip
the apple wedges in it.
5 About 6 minutes before the end
of cooking time for the chops, add
the apple wedges to the pan and fry
for 3 minutes on each side, until
soft and lightly browned on the
outside of the apple.
6 Using a fish slice, transfer the
chops to a warmed serving dish and
top with the apple wedges. Garnish
with parsley and serve at once.

Spaghetti with anchovy sauce

SERVES 4

500 g/1 lb spaghetti
salt
1 teaspoon vegetable oil
25 g/1 oz butter

ANCHOVY SAUCE
2 tablespoons vegetable oil
1 clove garlic, crushed (optional)
1 large onion, finely chopped
50 g/2 oz can anchovy fillets in oil,
mashed to a paste
2 teaspoons plain flour
400 g/14 oz can chopped tomatoes
2 teaspoons tomato purée
2 teaspoons dried basil
freshly ground black pepper

1 Bring a large pan of salted water to the boil, swirl in the oil and add the spaghetti. Bring back to the boil then lower the heat and simmer for 10-12 minutes or until the spaghetti is quite tender yet firm to the bite.

2 Meanwhile, make anchovy sauce: heat the oil in a heavy-based saucepan, add the garlic, if using, and onion and fry very gently for 7 minutes until golden.
3 Stir the anchovy paste and flour into the onion and cook, stirring, for a further 2 minutes. Gradually blend in the chopped tomatoes and their juices, the tomato purée and basil. Add pepper to taste and simmer gently for 8-10 minutes, stirring occasionally.
4 Drain the pasta thoroughly, then return to the rinsed-out pan. Add the butter and season well with pepper. Toss over gentle heat until spaghetti is coated in butter.
5 Transfer the spaghetti to warmed serving plates and top with the anchovy sauce. Serve at once. For a finishing touch, see Serving ideas.

Cook's Notes

TIME
Preparing and cooking the dish take less than 30 minutes in all.

WATCHPOINT
The anchovies are so salty it is wise not to use any salt when seasoning both the sauce and the spaghetti.

SERVING IDEAS
Sprinkle the top of each platter liberally with finely grated Parmesan cheese to give a true Italian flavour. Serve with a green salad for a good colour contrast.

 VARIATIONS
For a more substantial dish, a 200 g/7 oz can of tuna may be drained and flaked into the sauce during cooking. Chopped cocktail gherkins, drained capers or chopped, stoned olives may also be added at this stage.

●635 calories/2650 kj per portion

Smoked mackerel parcels

SERVES 4

 350 g/12 oz smoked mackerel, skinned, boned and flaked

 100 g/4 oz plain flour

salt

1 egg

700 ml/1¼ pints milk

25 g/1 oz lard

25 g/1 oz margarine or butter

25 g/1 oz cornflour (see Cook's tip)

pinch of ground mace

freshly ground white pepper

50 g/2 oz Cheddar cheese, grated

lemon slices, to garnish

1 Heat the oven to 200C/400F/Gas 6.
2 Make the pancakes: sift the plain flour and a pinch of salt into a bowl. Make a hollow in the centre and add the egg. Gradually mix in 300 ml/½ pint milk, beating well until the batter is smooth.
3 Melt a small amount of the lard in a frying-pan then pour in enough batter to coat the base of the pan. Cook for 1 minute until golden, then turn over and cook the other side.

Lift on to a sheet of greaseproof paper. Continue making pancakes, interleaving each with greaseproof paper until all the batter has been used, adding a little more lard each time. It will make 4-6 pancakes depending on size of pan used.
4 Melt the margarine in a saucepan, sprinkle in the cornflour and stir over low heat for 1-2 minutes until straw-coloured. Remove the sauce from the heat and very gradually stir in the remaining milk. Add the mace and season with salt and pepper. Return pan to the heat

and simmer, stirring until thick.
5 Put two-thirds of the sauce in a bowl and stir in the cheese. Set aside. Stir the flaked fish into the remaining sauce in the pan.
6 Lay the pancakes flat and divide the mixture between them, placing it in the centre of each. Fold the sides over the filling, then roll up to make a parcel.
7 Place in a shallow ovenproof dish and pour over the cheese sauce.
8 Bake in the oven for 25 minutes until the sauce is golden and bubbling. Serve the parcels at once.

Cook's Notes

TIME
20 minutes to prepare, plus about 40 minutes cooking time.

VARIATIONS
Any cooked smoked fish such as kippers, haddock or cod can be used for this recipe instead of the mackerel. Add 50 g/2 oz sliced mushrooms to the sauce and simmer for 5 minutes before adding the fish.

 FREEZING
To make this dish for freezing, cook in a greased foil dish. To serve: cover with foil and reheat from frozen in a 200C/400F/ Gas 6 oven for 30-35 minutes.

COOK'S TIP
Cornflour will make a very smooth sauce, but plain flour can be used.

●590 calories/2450 kj per portion

Spicy beef stir-fry

SERVES 4

350 g/12 oz braising steak, trimmed and cut into very thin strips (see Cook's tips)
2 teaspoons Worcestershire sauce
salt and freshly ground black pepper
600 ml/1 pint water
1 beef stock cube
1 small red or green pepper
250 g/9 oz courgettes
1 small onion
1 tablespoon vegetable oil
little soy sauce
green pepper and onion rings, to garnish (optional)

1 Put the strips of braising steak into a bowl with the Worcestershire sauce and season to taste with salt and pepper. Stir well and leave to stand for 10 minutes.

2 Pour the water into a saucepan, add the stock cube, then the meat. Bring to the boil, stirring until the stock cube has dissolved, then lower heat and simmer for about 1 hour or until meat is tender and liquid has almost evaporated. [!]

3 Meanwhile, prepare vegetables: first deseed the red pepper and cut into 2.5 cm/1 inch strips. Top and tail the courgettes and cut lengthways into thin sticks. Cut the onion in half and slice.

4 Heat oil in a wok or frying-pan, add the onion and fry for about 1 minute. Add red pepper and fry for a further minute, then add the courgettes and stir well.

5 Stir in the cooked beef and juices (see Variation). Mix them together well, cover and allow to fry for 2-3 minutes, then add soy sauce to taste (see Cook's tips). Transfer to a warmed serving dish, garnish with green pepper and onion rings, if liked, and serve at once.

Cook's Notes

TIME
Total preparation and cooking for the stir-fry is 1½ hours.

WATCHPOINT
Check the saucepan occasionally to ensure it does not become too dry. If necessary, add a little more water to the pan.

COOK'S TIPS
Use frozen braising steak and cut it while still frozen.

The soy sauce is salty, so no extra salt is necessary.

VARIATION
Add 250 g/9 oz beansprouts at stage 5 for a more substantial dish.

● 205 calories/850 kj per portion

Chicken and pasta salad

SERVES 4

350 g/12 oz cooked chicken, cubed
150 g/5 oz pasta shells
salt
1 teaspoon vegetable oil
150 ml/¼ pint soured cream
1 tablespoon capers
2 spring onions, chopped
1 tablespoon chopped fresh
  tarragon (see Variations)
salt and freshly ground black pepper
a little extra chopped tarragon, to
  garnish

1 Bring a large pan of salted water to the boil, swirl in the oil, then add the pasta. Bring back to the boil and cook for 7-10 minutes until tender.

2 Drain thoroughly, then rinse under cold running water to remove excess starch (see Cook's tip). Drain again and set aside until cold.

3 Mix all the other ingredients together thoroughly, with salt and pepper to taste and then stir in the pasta shells. Turn into a deep serving bowl, garnish with a sprinkling of tarragon. Serve cold.

Cook's Notes

TIME
Total preparation takes about 20 minutes.

SERVING IDEAS
Serve with a simple green or tomato salad.

COOK'S TIP
Rinsing the pasta under cold water also prevents it sticking together when cold.

VARIATIONS
If fresh tarragon is not available, use another fresh herb such as mint, parsley or chives.

For a more substantial dish, add a quartered hard-boiled egg per person.

Cold cooked fish may be used instead of cooked chicken.

● 325 calories/1350 kj per portion

Ham and cheese stuffed aubergines

SERVES 4

2 aubergines, each weighing about
  250 g/9 oz
salt
25 g/1 oz margarine or butter
1 onion, chopped
100 g/4 oz cooked ham, chopped
1 tomato, chopped
50 g/2 oz fresh white breadcrumbs
1 tablespoon chopped fresh parsley
100 g/4 oz mature Cheddar cheese,
  grated
freshly ground black pepper
1-2 tablespoons stock or water

1 Trim off stalk end of aubergines, cut aubergines in half lengthways and, leaving a 5 mm/¼ in thick shell, scoop out and reserve the flesh (see Preparation).
2 Bring a pan of salted water to the boil, add aubergine shells, lower heat and cook for 5 minutes. Lift out with a slotted spoon and drain aubergine shells upside down.

3 Heat the oven to 180C/350F/Gas 4.
4 Meanwhile, chop the reserved aubergine flesh. Melt the margarine in a frying-pan, add the onion and fry gently for 5 minutes until soft and lightly coloured. Add chopped aubergine and cook, stirring, for a further 5 minutes.
5 Remove from heat and mix in the ham, tomato, breadcrumbs, parsley and half the cheese. Season to taste with salt and pepper. Mix in just enough stock to lightly moisten the mixture.
6 Arrange the drained aubergine shells in a single layer in an oven-proof dish. Spoon the filling into the shells, dividing it equally between them and sprinkle with remaining cheese.
7 Bake in the oven for 25-30 minutes until the filling is hot and the cheese has melted. Serve at once straight from the dish.

Cook's Notes

 TIME
Preparation about 25 minutes, cooking in the oven takes 25-30 minutes.

 SERVING IDEAS
Serve the aubergines as a lunch or supper dish on their own. Or serve the aubergines as a dinner-party starter, sprinkled with chopped fresh parsley and garnished with sliced black olives.

●240 calories/1000 kj per portion

PREPARATION
To make the aubergine shells, follow diagram:

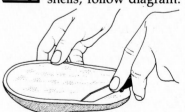

Use a small vegetable knife to mark a line 5 mm/¼ inch in from the skin, then use a metal spoon to scoop out the centre flesh.

Spicy lamb chops

SERVES 4

12 breakfast or thin-cut lamb
   chops, each weighing about
   25-50 g/1-2 oz, defrosted
   if frozen
juice of 1 lemon
1 teaspoon salt
1 clove garlic, crushed (optional)
1 onion, finely chopped
1 teaspoon ground coriander
½ teaspoon ground ginger
¼ teaspoon chilli powder or
   seasoning
¼ teaspoon sweet paprika
150 g/5 oz natural yoghurt
lime or lemon wedges and extra
   sweet paprika, to garnish

1 Put the chops on a board then, using a small sharp knife, make several slits in each. Sprinkle the chops with a little of the lemon juice and all the salt.

2 Mix the remaining lemon juice with the garlic, if using, the onion, coriander, ginger, chilli powder, paprika and yoghurt.

3 Arrange the chops in a single layer in a shallow dish and spread with half the yoghurt mixture. Turn the chops over and coat with the remaining yoghurt mixture. Cover and leave to marinate for at least 4 hours in a cool place.

4 Heat the grill to high.

5 Remove chops from the dish and arrange in a single layer on the grill rack. Grill for 3-4 minutes on each side or until cooked through. Garnish with lime wedges and serve.

Cook's Notes

 TIME
Preparation 15 minutes; marinating 4 hours or overnight; grilling 8 minutes.

 SERVING IDEAS
These tasty chops can be eaten with the fingers.

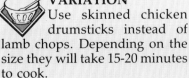 **VARIATION**
Use skinned chicken drumsticks instead of lamb chops. Depending on the size they will take 15-20 minutes to cook.

● 240 calories/1000 kj per portion

Gingered chicken livers

SERVES 4

500 g/1 lb chicken livers
2 teaspoons cornflour
1 teaspoon ground ginger (see Variation)
½ teaspoon caster sugar
2 tablespoons tomato puree
2 tablespoons soy sauce
2 tablespoons medium sherry
4 tablespoons orange juice
150 ml/¼ pint chicken stock
2 tablespoons vegetable oil
1 onion, cut into eighths and separated into 'leaves'
3 celery stalks, sliced diagonally into 1 cm/½ inch pieces
1 large green pepper, deseeded and cut into 1 cm/½ inch strips
100 g/4 oz button mushrooms, sliced

1 Put the cornflour in a small bowl with the ginger and sugar and mix in the tomato purée. Stir in the soy sauce, sherry, orange juice and stock and set aside.

2 Heat the oil in a large frying-pan or a wok. Add the onion and celery and stir-fry over moderate heat for 1 minute. Add the pepper strips and stir-fry for a further 2 minutes, then add the mushrooms and chicken livers and stir-fry for a further 3-4 minutes, until the livers are evenly browned.

3 Pour the soy sauce mixture into the pan and bring to the boil. Lower the heat and simmer, stirring, for about 5 minutes, or until the chicken livers are cooked through (see Cook's tip). Serve at once.

Cook's Notes

TIME
Preparation takes 15-20 minutes, cooking takes about 25 minutes.

SERVING IDEAS
Serve individual portions in a ring of boiled or steamed rice.

VARIATION
Omit the ground ginger and caster sugar and add instead 2 pieces stem ginger, sliced thinly then cut into strips, and 1 tablespoon ginger syrup.

COOK'S TIP
Chicken livers need very little cooking. They are ready when they are no longer bloody but still pink inside.

● 285 calories/1175 kj per portion

Streaky pork with mandarin sauce

SERVES 4

500 g/1 lb lean belly of pork
   rashers, rind, bones and excess
   fat removed, and cut in half
   across (see Buying guide)
1 tablespoon vegetable oil
1 large onion, sliced
300 g/11 oz can mandarin orange
   segments, drained with juice
   reserved
about 150 ml/¼ pint chicken stock
¼ teaspoon ground ginger
1 tablespoon lemon juice or vinegar
1 green pepper, deseeded and
   chopped
salt and freshly ground black pepper
1 tablespoon cornflour
2 tablespoons water

1 Heat the oil in a large frying-pan. Add the pork and fry over moderate heat for 5 minutes turning, until brown on both sides.

2 Add the onion to the pan and fry for a further 5 minutes until the onion is soft. Pour off excess fat from the pan.

3 Make up the reserved fruit juice to 300 ml/½ pint with the chicken stock and pour into the pan. Add the ginger, lemon juice and green pepper and season to taste with salt and pepper. Bring to the boil, then lower the heat, cover, and simmer for 30-40 minutes until the pork is cooked (the juices run clear when the meat is pierced with a skewer).

4 Remove from the heat (see Cook's tip). Blend the cornflour with the water, then stir in a little of the liquid from the pan. Pour back into the pan and bring to the boil, stirring constantly, then simmer for 3 minutes until the liquid is thick and has a smooth consistency. ⚠ Add the mandarin orange segments and stir carefully to coat in sauce.

5 Turn into a warmed serving dish and serve at once.

Cook's Notes

TIME
Preparation takes 20 minutes; cooking takes about 40 minutes.

BUYING GUIDE
Belly of pork is sold in supermarkets cut into rashers and is often labelled 'streaky pork rashers'. If buying from the butcher, ask him to cut the belly of pork into rashers.

⚠ WATCHPOINT
The sauce should be of a coating consistency. If it gets too thick, however, add some remaining chicken stock.

COOK'S TIP
Belly of pork is a fatty meat. If liked, blot the surface of the sauce with some absorbent paper to remove the excess fat at this stage.

VARIATION
Use a 225 g/8 oz can pineapple pieces instead of the mandarins.

SERVING IDEAS
For a delicious supper dish, serve with plain boiled rice and a mixed salad.

● 380 calories/1500 kj per portion

Stir-fry chicken

SERVES 4

275 g/10 oz boneless raw chicken, cut into bite-sized pieces
2 tablespoons soy sauce
1 tablespoon sherry or water
¼ teaspoon ground ginger
2 teaspoons cornflour
2 tablespoons vegetable oil
3 spring onions, trimmed and sliced
1 small green pepper, deseeded and diced
100 g/4 oz mushrooms, chopped
½ small or ¼ large cauliflower, divided into about 10 florets
4 tablespoons water, or chicken stock if available
salt
2 tomatoes, sliced

1 In a bowl, mix together the soy sauce, sherry, ginger and cornflour. Stir in the chicken pieces and coat evenly in the mixture.

2 Heat 1 tablespoon oil in a large frying-pan or wok over moderate heat until very hot, then stir-fry the meat for 1 minute, turning it constantly. Transfer the meat to a plate and keep it warm in a low oven.

3 Heat the remaining oil over moderate heat until very hot. Add the spring onions, green pepper, mushrooms and cauliflower and stir-fry for 1 minute. Add the water or stock and cook for 2-3 minutes.

4 Return the chicken to the pan. Season with salt. Stir in the tomatoes and heat through over moderate heat for 1 minute. Serve at once.

Cook's Notes

TIME
A quick dish that takes 25 minutes.

COOK'S TIP
For stir-frying the Chinese use a wok — a metal pan with sloping sides. The principle of stir-frying is to cook quickly over high heat, so the oil must be hot and the ingredients small.

● 140 calories/600 kj per portion

Buckling and beetroot salad

SERVES 4

2 buckling (see Buying guide)

10 cm/4 inch piece of cucumber

250 g/9 oz cooked beetroot, cut into 5 mm/¼ inch rounds and then into neat strips

2 teaspoons vegetable oil

1 teaspoon cider or white wine vinegar

12 lettuce leaves, to serve

4 gherkins, cut into fan shapes and 4 sprigs of watercress, to garnish

1 Remove the skin from the buckling and carefully pick the flesh from the bones. Flake the flesh into a large bowl. If the fish has roes, cut these into neat pieces and add them to the flesh.

2 Cut the piece of cucumber across into 4 equal slices, then cut each slice into strips.

3 Add the cucumber and the remaining ingredients, except the lettuce and gherkins and watercress, to the buckling and toss together lightly with a fork.

4 Arrange lettuce leaves on each of 4 individual serving plates. Pile the buckling mixture into the centre. Garnish salad with a gherkin fan and watercress and serve at once.

Cook's Notes

 TIME
This tasty and colourful salad takes only about 10 minutes to prepare.

 SERVING IDEAS
Serve this salad as an unusual light lunch.

BUYING GUIDE
Buckling are smoked herrings and can be bought from fishmongers, supermarkets and delicatessens.

● 195 calories/800 kj per portion

70

Beefy spaghetti bake

SERVES 4

350 g/12 oz minced beef
100 g/4 oz spaghetti, broken into
   short lengths
25 g/1 oz dripping
2 medium onions, chopped
225 g/8 oz can tomatoes
1 teaspoon dried mixed herbs
salt and freshly ground black
   pepper
1 tablespoon vegetable oil
25 g/1 oz butter
2 tablespoons grated Parmesan
   cheese

SAUCE

1 egg, beaten
25 g/1 oz plain flour
300 ml/½ pint milk
50 g/2 oz Cheddar cheese, grated

TOPPING

25 g/1 oz dried breadcrumbs
50 g/2 oz Cheddar cheese, grated
25 g/1 oz butter

1 Melt the dripping in a frying-pan, add the onions and fry gently until soft. Add the minced beef and fry over moderate heat until well browned, stirring constantly to break up lumps. Stir in the tomatoes, herbs and salt and pepper to taste and continue cooking for a further 10-15 minutes.

2 Meanwhile, bring a pan of salted water to the boil, stir in the oil, then add the spaghetti. Cook at a rolling boil for 10-12 minutes until the spaghetti is just tender. Drain thoroughly.

3 Heat the oven to 190C/375F/Gas 5.

4 Melt the butter in the rinsed-out pan, add the spaghetti and Parmesan cheese and toss well to mix over gentle heat.

5 Put half the spaghetti in the bottom of a buttered ovenproof dish. Spread the meat mixture evenly on top, then add the remaining spaghetti.

6 Make the sauce: mix the egg and flour together in a small saucepan, then gradually stir in the milk and Cheddar cheese.

7 Place the pan over gentle heat and heat through for about 5 minutes

until thickened, whisking constantly and vigorously all the time with a wire whisk. Add salt and pepper to taste, then pour over the spaghetti.

8 To make the topping: sprinkle the breadcrumbs and cheese over the top of the sauce, then dot with the butter. Bake in the oven for about 20 minutes until the topping is golden brown. Serve hot.

Cook's Notes

 TIME
Preparation time will be about 30 minutes plus 20 minutes baking in the oven.

 COOK'S TIPS
You can make this dish with left-over minced beef or lamb, in which case the meat will only need a few minutes browning to warm it through and give it colour.

Adding oil to spaghetti during the cooking helps to prevent the pasta sticking together.

When making a white sauce by this quick all-in-one method, a wire balloon whisk is more efficient than a wooden spoon for beating out any lumps.

 SERVING IDEAS
Serve this dish with crusty French bread and butter, and a green salad tossed in French dressing.

 VARIATION
To make it easier to serve, the spaghetti is broken into short lengths before cooking. Alternatively, you could use macaroni or small pasta bows or shells.

● 740 calories/3100 kj per portion

Sherried chicken livers

SERVES 4

500 g/1 lb chicken livers, defrosted
   if frozen and quartered (see
   Buying guide)
2 tablespoons vegetable oil
100 g/4 oz onion, chopped
50 g/2 oz cooked ham, chopped
100 g/4 oz mushrooms, sliced
1 teaspoon ground sage

SAUCE

25 g/1 oz margarine or butter
2 tablespoons plain flour
150 ml/¼ pint chicken stock
1 tablespoon lemon juice
1 teaspoon made English mustard
3 tablespoons medium dry sherry
salt and freshly ground black pepper
1 crisp lettuce, shredded, to serve

1 Heat the oil in a frying-pan. Add the onion, ham and mushrooms and cook gently for 5 minutes until the onion is soft and lightly coloured.

2 Add the chicken livers and sage. Lower the heat and cook very gently for 15 minutes, or until the livers are cooked through but still pink in the middle, stirring from time to time to prevent sticking.

3 Meanwhile, make the sauce: melt the margarine in a small saucepan, sprinkle in the flour and stir over low heat for 1-2 minutes until straw-coloured. Gradually stir in the chicken stock, lemon juice and mustard, bring to the boil and simmer gently, until thick and smooth. Stir in the sherry.

4 Pour the sauce over the prepared livers, mix together well, then season to taste with salt and pepper.

5 To serve: arrange the lettuce in the base of a serving dish. Spoon the liver mixture on top and serve.

Noodles napolitana

SERVES 4

250 g/9 oz ribbon noodles
1 tablespoon vegetable oil
1 large onion, finely chopped
175 g/6 oz mushrooms
225 g/8 oz back bacon, rinds
  removed, chopped
3 celery stalks, chopped
1 large clove garlic, crushed
  (optional)
2 tablespoons tomato purée
175 ml/6 fl oz chicken stock
1 teaspoon dried oregano
salt and freshly ground black pepper
15 g/½ oz butter
1 tablespoon grated Parmesan
  cheese, to serve

Cook's Notes

TIME
15 minutes preparation,
cooking 10 minutes.

COOK'S TIP
The sauce can be made a
day ahead and stored in
the refrigerator.

DID YOU KNOW
Oregano is the wild
form of the Mediterra-
nean herb marjoram, and has a
more pungent flavour, particularly when dried. Oregano is
widely used in Italian cooking
and even a little gives a typically
Italian flavour to such dishes as
spaghetti or pizza.

FREEZING
Only the sauce can be
frozen. After complet-
ing stage 2, place the sauce in a
rigid container, cover, label and
freeze. Store for up to 6 months.
To serve: reheat from frozen
over low heat, adding a little
stock to moisten. Continue from
stage 3.

VARIATIONS
Use cooked chicken or
turkey in place of bacon.

●565 calories/2475 kj per portion

1 Heat the oil in a frying-pan over moderate heat. Add the onion, mushrooms, bacon and celery and fry for 3 minutes, stirring from time to time.
2 Add garlic if using, tomato purée, stock and oregano to the pan. Season well with salt and pepper, lower the heat and simmer for 5 minutes until thickened. ✳

3 Cook the noodles in plenty of boiling salted water for 5 minutes or until just tender. Drain and return to the rinsed-out pan, then toss with the butter.
4 Turn the noodles on to a hot serving dish and top with the bacon and mushroom mixture. Sprinkle with grated Parmesan cheese and serve at once.

Lamb and apricot salad

SERVES 4
350 g/12 oz cooked lamb, diced
400 g/14 oz can apricot halves,
  drained and chopped
150 ml/¼ pint thick bottled
  mayonnaise
4 tablespoons natural yoghurt
1 tablespoon clear honey
2 teaspoons finely grated lemon
  zest
½ teaspoon ground cinnamon
salt and freshly ground black pepper
350 g/12 oz potatoes, boiled and
  roughly chopped
1 small lettuce
25 g/1 oz toasted flaked almonds

1 Put the mayonnaise in a large bowl and stir in the yoghurt, honey, lemon zest and cinnamon. Season to taste with salt and pepper, then cover and refrigerate for 30 minutes (see Cook's tip).
2 Mix together the lamb, potatoes and apricots and gently fold into the mayonnaise mixture.
3 Arrange the lettuce leaves in a bowl or shallow dish. Spoon the salad into the centre and sprinkle the almonds over the top. Serve the salad at once.

Cook's Notes

TIME
Preparation is about 10 minutes, but allow 30 minutes for chilling.

VARIATIONS
Use canned mandarins or pineapple instead of the apricots, and chicken, ham or tongue instead of the lamb. Substitute 250 g/9 oz cooked rice for the boiled potatoes. If cooking the rice especially for this dish, you will need 75 g/3 oz of raw rice.

COOK'S TIP Chilling the mayonnaise mixture improves the flavour but is not essential.

●575 calories/2400 kj per portion

Surprise terrine

SERVES 6

250 g/9 oz chicken livers
250 g/9 oz boneless belly pork, rind removed
1 small onion, cut into chunks
250 g/9 oz minced beef
1 tablespoon tomato purée
½ teaspoon dried oregano
1 clove garlic, crushed (optional)
3 tablespoons red wine (see Economy)
salt and freshly ground black pepper
100 g/4 oz stuffed olives
3 bay leaves
1 tablespoon chopped parsley, to garnish

1 Heat the oven to 180C/350F/Gas 4.
2 Wash and trim the livers, removing any discoloured parts with a sharp knife.
3 Mince the livers, pork and onion finely in a mincer or chop finely in a food processor (see Cook's tip). Place in a large bowl and stir in the minced beef, tomato purée, oregano, garlic, if using, and wine. Mix thoroughly and season generously with salt and pepper.
4 Reserve 3 of the olives for garnish, then halve the rest. Spoon half of the terrine mixture into a 700 ml/1¼ pint deep rectangular dish or tin. Arrange the halved olives in the dish (see Preparation).
5 Carefully spoon the remaining terrine mixture on top of the olives and arrange the bay leaves on top. Tap the base of dish a few times on a work surface so the mixture fills the gaps between the olives. Cover the dish loosely with foil.
6 Put the dish into a roasting tin, pour in boiling water to come halfway up the sides of the dish and cook in the oven for about 1½ hours. To test for doneness, tilt the dish and if the juices run clear the terrine is cooked. Remove the dish from the roasting tin and cover the surface of the terrine with foil. Put heavy weights on top, leave to cool, then refrigerate overnight.
7 To serve: turn the terrine out on to a platter. Slice the reserved olives and arrange them down the centre of the terrine. Sprinkle a row of chopped parsley either side.

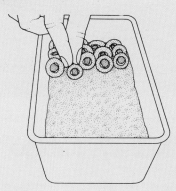

Kidneys turbigo

SERVES 4

 6 lamb kidneys, skinned and
    halved with cores removed

 20 small onions, unpeeled, total
    weight about 175-225 g/6-8 oz
    (see Variation)

50 g/2 oz butter

6 pork chipolata sausages

100 g/4 oz button mushrooms,
    halved

2 teaspoons plain flour

225 ml/8 fl oz beef stock

1 tablespoon medium sherry

1 teaspoon tomato purée

1 bay leaf

salt and freshly ground black pepper

1 tablespoon chopped fresh
    parsley, to garnish

CROUTES

3 slices white bread, crusts
    removed, quartered diagonally

vegetable oil, for frying

1 Put the small unpeeled onions
into a small saucepan and pour in
cold water to cover. Bring to the boil
and boil for 2 minutes. Drain, rinse
under cold running water, then
drain again. Using a small, sharp
knife, peel the onions and trim the
root ends. Set aside.

2 Cut the kidney halves in half
crossways.

3 Melt the butter in a large frying-
pan. When it is foaming, add the
kidneys and fry over brisk heat for 1
minute on each side. Using a slotted
spoon, transfer the kidneys to a
plate while frying the sausages.

4 Add the sausages to the pan and
fry over moderate heat for 3-4 minutes, turning to brown evenly.
Using a slotted spoon, remove
sausages from the pan. Cut each
sausage into 3 pieces, then add to
the kidneys.

5 Add the onions and mushrooms
to the pan and fry over brisk heat
for 2 minutes. Sprinkle in flour and
stir over low heat for 1-2 minutes.

Gradually stir in the beef stock,
then add the sherry and tomato
purée. Bring to the boil, stirring.
Lower the heat and return the kidneys, sausages and any juices from
the plate to the pan, together with
the bay leaf and salt and pepper.

6 Cover the pan and simmer very
gently for 20-25 minutes, until the
kidneys are tender.

7 A few minutes before the kidneys
are ready, make the croûtes: pour
oil into a frying-pan to a depth of
5 mm/¼ inch; heat, then add the
bread triangles and fry, until golden
brown on both sides. Drain on
absorbent paper.

8 Transfer the kidney mixture to a
warmed serving dish and sprinkle
with chopped parsley. Arrange the
croûtes round edge. Serve at once.

Cook's Notes

 TIME
Preparation takes 25
minutes; cooking about
25-30 minutes.

VARIATION
If button onions (some-
times known as pick-
ling onions) are unavailable,
use 2 ordinary onions, sliced
5 mm/¼ inch thick, unblanched.

SERVING IDEAS
Serve with boiled rice
and a green salad.

This classic kidney dish is
traditionally garnished with
fried bread *croûtes*, a larger version of croûtons. *Croûtes* may be
dipped in finely chopped parsley, to give a pretty finish.

●500 calories/2100 kj per portion

Egg and bacon spaghetti

SERVES 4

350 g/12 oz spaghetti (see Variation)
4 eggs
75 g/3 oz Parmesan cheese, grated
freshly ground black pepper
salt
1 tablespoon olive oil
225 g/8 oz streaky bacon rashers,
    rinds removed and cut into
    narrow strips (see Buying guide)
½ dried red chilli pepper (optional)

1 Beat the eggs in a bowl, then stir in two-thirds of the Parmesan cheese and plenty of pepper. Set aside.

2 Bring a pan of salted water to the boil and cook the spaghetti for about 10 minutes until *al dente* (tender, yet firm to the bite).

3 Meanwhile, heat the oil in a large frying-pan and add the bacon strips and chilli pepper, if using. Fry over high heat until the bacon is crisp and beginning to brown. Discard the chilli pepper, if used.

4 Drain the spaghetti well, then add to the frying-pan and quickly fork it round to mix with the oil and bacon.

Remove the pan from the heat.

5 Pour the egg and cheese mixture over the spaghetti in the pan and quickly fork through. Turn the spaghetti into a warmed serving dish and grind more black pepper over the top. Hand the remaining Parmesan cheese separately.

Cook's Notes

TIME
Preparation and cooking take only about 20 minutes.

VARIATION
Try this dish with whole-wheat spaghetti, but allow 15-20 minutes cooking time.

BUYING GUIDE
If you can buy streaky bacon in one piece instead of rashers, cut it into small dice: this is how the Italians would prepare the bacon for this favourite spaghetti dish.

! WATCHPOINT
Be sure to remove the frying-pan from the heat before adding the egg and cheese mixture. The heat from the pan will be enough just to cook and thicken the egg slightly without allowing it to scramble.

●740 calories/3100 kj per portion

Saucy ham and prawn rolls

SERVES 4

8 slices cooked ham, total weight 250 g/9 oz
100 g/4 oz packet parsley and thyme stuffing mix
50 g/2 oz peeled prawns, defrosted if frozen, chopped
parsley sprigs, to garnish

CHEESE SAUCE

75 g/3 oz Cheddar cheese, grated
25 g/1 oz margarine or butter
25 g/1 oz plain flour
300 ml/½ pint milk
pinch of freshly grated nutmeg
½ teaspoon made English mustard
salt and freshly ground black pepper

1 Heat the oven to 200C/400F/Gas 6.
2 Make the stuffing according to packet instructions. Allow to cool slightly and mix in the prawns.

3 Divide the stuffing between the ham slices, spooning it in a strip about 1 cm/1½ inch from one edge. Starting at the edge nearest the stuffing, carefully roll up each slice of ham. Place the prawn-filled ham rolls, with the join side down, in a shallow ovenproof dish large enough to hold them in a single layer.
4 Make the sauce: melt margarine in a saucepan, sprinkle in the flour and stir over low heat for 1-2 minutes until straw-coloured. Remove from heat and gradually stir in the milk. Add the nutmeg and mustard and season to taste with salt and pepper. Return to the heat and simmer, stirring, until thick and smooth. Remove the pan from the heat and stir in half the grated Cheddar cheese.
5 Pour the sauce over the ham rolls and sprinkle with the remaining cheese. Bake in the oven for 20 minutes until the sauce is golden and bubbling. Garnish with parsley and serve at once straight from the dish (see Serving ideas).

Cook's Notes

TIME
Preparing the rolls takes about 20 minutes plus 20 minutes cooking.

VARIATIONS
Use slices of roast pork instead of the ham.
If preferred, make your own stuffing with 75 g/3 oz cooked rice (you will need 25 g/1 oz raw rice), chopped celery, green pepper and mushrooms.
For a stronger flavoured sauce use Gruyère cheese instead of Cheddar.

SERVING IDEAS
To make a substantial supper dish, serve with a green vegetable such as French beans or broccoli and crusty bread and butter.

●380 calories/1600 kj per portion

Spinach buckwheat pancakes

SERVES 4

350 g/12 oz fresh spinach, stalks and large midribs removed
50 g/2 oz plain flour
50 g/2 oz buckwheat flour
salt
300 ml/½ pint milk
1 egg, beaten
1 tablespoon vegetable oil
100 g/4 oz cooked ham, chopped
100 g/4 oz cottage cheese, sieved
freshly ground black pepper
vegetable oil, for frying

1 Mix the flours and a pinch of salt in a bowl, then make a well in the centre. Gradually add the milk, stirring the flour in with a wooden spoon, then add the egg and oil. Whisk together to make a batter.

2 Brush a large heavy-based frying-pan with oil and place over moderate heat until hot. Remove from the heat and pour in sufficient batter to coat the base of the pan thinly.

3 Return the pan to the heat and cook until the top of the pancake looks dry and the underside is golden brown. Loosen the edge with a palette knife and shake the pan, then turn the pancake over and cook on the other side for a further 20-30 seconds. Lift on to a sheet of greaseproof paper and keep warm.

4 Make 3 more pancakes in the same way, brushing the pan with oil each time and interleaving with greaseproof paper.

5 Put the spinach in a large sauce-pan with just the water that adheres to the leaves after washing. Sprinkle over ½ teaspoon salt and cook over moderate heat for about 10 minutes.

6 Drain the spinach well and chop finely. Place it in a bowl and mix it with the ham and cottage cheese. Season with salt and pepper.

7 Place an equal amount of the spinach mixture in centre of each pancake. Fold opposite flaps over the filling, then fold over the other two flaps to make a parcel.

8 Heat a little more oil in the frying-pan, add the pancakes and warm through over gentle heat for 4-6 minutes, turning once. Transfer to a warmed serving dish and serve.

Cook's Notes

TIME
Preparation and cooking take about 25 minutes.

SERVING IDEAS
These pancakes need very little accompaniment. Serve with a salad and garnish with tomatoes and olives.

VARIATIONS
Use 250 g/9 oz frozen spinach instead of fresh spinach. Chopped fried bacon may be substituted for the ham.

DID YOU KNOW
Buckwheat flour, available in health food shops, has dark flecks and a distinctive rich flavour and slightly gritty texture.

It gets its name from the Dutch *boek-weit* which means beechnut (buckwheat grains are shaped like beechnuts). The grains are the fruit of a herbaceous plant belonging to the rhubarb, dock and sorrel family.

● 295 calories/1225 kj per portion

Gammon with raisin sauce

SERVES 4

4 gammon rashers, about 5 mm/¼ inch thick
1-2 tablespoons melted margarine or butter
4 small bananas

RAISIN SAUCE
100 g/4 oz dark soft brown sugar
good pinch of salt
good pinch of ground cloves
½ teaspoon ground cinnamon
2 tablespoons vinegar
75 g/3 oz seedless raisins
200 ml/7 fl oz cider
25 g/1 oz margarine or butter
1 tablespoon cornflour
finely grated zest and juice of 1 small orange

1 Make the raisin sauce: put the sugar in a small saucepan, add the salt, cloves, cinnamon, vinegar, raisins and cider. Bring to the boil, then lower the heat and stir in the margarine.

2 Blend the cornflour with a little of the orange zest and juice, then stir in the remainder. When the margarine has melted, remove the pan from the heat and quickly stir in the cornflour mixture. Return to the heat, bring back to the boil and simmer gently for 2 minutes, stirring constantly. Remove from the heat and cover the surface of the sauce closely with cling film while cooking the gammon.

3 Heat grill to moderate. Trim rind off gammon, if liked, then snip the fat (see Preparation). Arrange the rashers on the grill rack and brush with a little melted margarine. Grill for about 5 minutes, then turn the rashers over and continue grilling for a further 5 minutes or until tender and cooked through.

4 Meanwhile, peel the bananas, and thinly slice them. Arrange the slices on top of each gammon rasher. Brush well with melted margarine and grill for a further 2 minutes.

5 Uncover the sauce and reheat gently, stirring vigorously. Transfer the gammon and bananas to a hot serving dish. Drizzle over a little of the raisin sauce, then pour the remainder into a warmed sauceboat and hand separately.

Cook's Notes

TIME
Preparation and cooking about 30 minutes.

SERVING IDEAS
Serve with peas and freshly cooked pasta shapes.

VARIATIONS
Spread slices of cooked ham with a little made mustard, wrap around halved bananas and arrange in a baking dish. Pour prepared raisin sauce over top and place under a moderate grill until heated through.

● 490 calories/2025 kj per portion

PREPARATION
To prepare the gammon rashers:

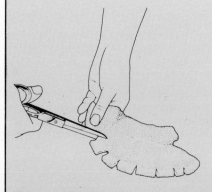

Trim rind off rashers, if liked, then, using sharp kitchen scissors, snip the fat at regular intervals to prevent it curling up during cooking.

Chef's layered salad

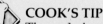

SERVES 4

8 lettuce leaves, shredded
4 hard-boiled eggs, sliced
4 tomatoes, sliced
275 g/10 oz boneless cooked
   chicken, diced (see Economy)
¼ small cucumber (about 5 cm/2
   inch), unpeeled and thinly sliced
1 large carrot, grated
100 g/4 oz Cheddar or Edam cheese,
   grated

DRESSING

4 tablespoons olive oil
1 tablespoon cider vinegar
salt and freshly ground black pepper

1 Arrange the shredded lettuce in the base of a large glass bowl (see Serving ideas).

2 Arrange the sliced eggs on the lettuce and then sliced tomatoes in a third layer over the eggs.

3 Place the diced chicken on top, then add layers of cucumber, carrot and finally grated cheese. When you arrange the cheese, leave a 2 cm/1 inch border of carrot showing around the edge.

4 Make the dressing: mix the oil and vinegar together and season to taste with salt and pepper. Pour evenly over the salad and serve at once.

Jansson's temptation

SERVES 4-6

 750 g/1½ lb potatoes
 40 g/1½ oz butter
2 medium onions, thinly sliced
45 g/1¾ oz can anchovy fillets,
   drained and soaked in milk for
   20 minutes
2 pickled herring fillets
300 ml/½ pint single cream
salt and freshly ground black pepper
1-2 tablespoons chopped parsley, to
   garnish
butter, for greasing

1 Heat the oven to 180C/350F/Gas 4.
2 Slice potatoes into matchstick lengths. Rinse and leave in cold water until needed, then drain thoroughly and pat dry with absorbent paper.
3 Melt 25 g/1 oz of the butter in a saucepan, add the onions and fry gently until light brown.
4 Meanwhile, drain the milk from the anchovies and dry them on absorbent paper. Rinse the herring fillets in cold water, dry them and cut into thin strips about 5 cm/2 inches long.
5 Arrange about half the potatoes over the base of a buttered oven-proof dish. Scatter the fried onions over the potatoes and top with half the fish. Cover with the remaining potatoes and arrange the rest of the fish on top in a lattice pattern. Dot with the remaining butter.
6 Season half the cream with pepper and a very little salt, then pour over the top.
7 Bake in the oven for 1 hour, then pour over the remaining cream and mix in with a fork. Return the dish to the oven for a further 30 minutes or until the potatoes are tender when pierced with a skewer. Sprinkle with the parsley and serve at once.

Cook's Notes

TIME
Preparation and cooking take about 2 hours.

SERVING IDEAS
This delicious Swedish dish is traditionally served as an appetizer, but makes a tasty snack at any time.

DID YOU KNOW
There are many theories about Jansson's identity and his particular temptation. One of the most popular reveals that he was Erik Jansson, a Swedish prophet of the 19th century. Despite being a committed vegetarian, it seems he was unable to resist this fish and potato dish—a perpetual reminder of his weakness.

●375 calories/1550 kj per portion

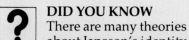

Chicken and yoghurt curry

SERVES 4

2 large chicken breasts, each weighing 250 g/9 oz, skinned and cut into 1 cm/½ inch pieces
25 g/1 oz margarine or butter
1 tablespoon vegetable or olive oil
1 large onion, chopped
1 clove garlic, crushed (optional)
1½ teaspoons ground ginger
2 teaspoons garam masala (see Variations)
150 ml/¼ pint chicken stock
150 g/5 oz natural yoghurt
½ cucumber, cut into 1 cm/½ inch pieces
40 g/1½ oz roasted salted peanuts (see Watchpoint)
coriander or parsley sprigs, to garnish

1 Heat the margarine and oil in a large frying-pan, add the onion and garlic, if using, and fry gently for 5 minutes until soft and lightly coloured. Stir in the spices and cook for a further 2 minutes.

2 Add the chicken and fry over moderate heat until sealed on all sides. Mix in the stock, bring to the boil, then lower the heat and simmer, uncovered, for 20 minutes or until the chicken is cooked.

3 Turn the heat to very low, then stir the yoghurt into the pan. Heat gently until warmed through, stirring constantly. Remove from the heat and mix in the cucumber.

4 Divide the mixture equally between 4 small bowls and sprinkle a few peanuts on top of each. Garnish with coriander or parsley sprigs and serve at once.

Cook's Notes

TIME
This dish takes only 30-40 minutes to prepare and cook.

VARIATIONS
To make your own garam masala for this recipe use 1 teaspoon ground cumin, ½ teaspoon ground chilli powder, ½ teaspoon ground turmeric and a large pinch of ground cinnamon. Mix well together.

Replace the cucumber with 2 thinly sliced courgettes, added to the pan with the chicken.

SERVING IDEAS
Serve with halved pitta bread, lightly toasted on both sides, and a selection of chutneys or pickles, such as mango chutney and lime pickle. Sliced bananas sprinkled with lemon juice make a good side dish to offset the hot curry.

WATCHPOINT
Roasted salted peanuts give a good flavour to this curry so do not add extra salt or it will be too salty.

●305 calories/1275 kj per portion

French onion flan

SERVES 4-6

750 g/1½ lb onions, finely sliced
225 g/8 oz shortcrust pastry,
  defrosted if frozen
40 g/1½ oz butter
2 tablespoons vegetable oil
egg white, for glazing (optional)
225 ml/8 fl oz single cream
3 egg yolks
½ teaspoon freshly grated nutmeg
salt and freshly ground black pepper

1 Heat the oven to 200C/400F/Gas 6.
2 Roll out the pastry on a floured surface and use to line a 23 cm/9 inch loose-bottomed flan tin or flan ring standing on a baking sheet. Prick the pastry base all over with a fork, then refrigerate for about 30 minutes.

3 Meanwhile, heat the butter with the oil in a large frying-pan and add the onions. Stir them round well, then cover the pan and leave to fry gently for about 30 minutes on a very low heat, stirring from time to time until they are soft and golden.
4 Line the pastry case with greaseproof paper or foil and weight it down with baking beans or rice. Bake in the oven for 10 minutes.
5 Remove the greaseproof paper and the beans, and brush the inside of the pastry with beaten egg white, if wished. Return the flan tin to the oven and bake for a further 5 minutes. Remove from the oven and set aside. Reduce the oven temperature to 180C/350F/Gas 4.
6 Mix the cream and egg yolks together in a bowl, stir in the nutmeg and season to taste with salt and pepper.
7 Spoon the cooked onions into the prepared pastry case and pour over the egg and cream mixture.

8 Bake in the oven for 35 minutes until the filling is set, then remove from the oven and leave to stand for at least 5-10 minutes. Remove the tin and place the flan on a serving plate. Serve warm or cold.

Country goulash

SERVES 4

2 onions, sliced
2 tablespoons vegetable oil
2 carrots, sliced
2 celery stalks, sliced
2 courgettes, sliced
1 green pepper, deseeded and
  diced
50 g/2 oz mushrooms, sliced
500 g/1 lb hard white cabbage,
  finely shredded
400 g/14 oz can tomatoes
1 tablespoon tomato purée
1 teaspoon lemon juice
300 ml/½ pint water
4½ teaspoons sweet paprika
1 tablespoon caraway seeds
salt and freshly ground black pepper
150 ml/¼ pint soured cream

Cook's Notes

TIME
Preparation and cooking the goulash take about 55 minutes.

SERVING IDEAS
Serve as a vegetarian meal with hot granary rolls. Or serve as an accompaniment to hot salt beef.

COOK'S TIP
Paprika loses colour when exposed to strong light. Store it in a cool, dark place to preserve the bright red colour which adds greatly to the distinctive appearance and taste of this dish.

● 235 calories/975 kj per portion

1 Heat the oil in a large saucepan, add the onions, carrots and celery and fry for about 5 minutes until soft and lightly coloured.

2 Add courgettes, green pepper, mushrooms and white cabbage and cook over moderate heat for 10 minutes, stirring occasionally to prevent the vegetables sticking to the saucepan.

3 Stir in the tomatoes with their juices, the tomato purée, lemon juice and water. Sprinkle in the paprika and caraway seeds and season well with salt and pepper.

4 Cover the pan and simmer for 20 minutes or until the vegetables are just tender. Taste and add more seasoning if necessary.

5 Transfer the goulash to a hot serving dish and spoon over the soured cream. Serve at once.

Egg and avocado bake

SERVES 6

6 eggs, separated
1 large avocado
6 tablespoons browned
 breadcrumbs (see Preparation)
3 tablespoons vegetable oil
1 onion, finely chopped
1 clove garlic, crushed (optional)
4 tablespoons finely chopped fresh
 parsley
salt and freshly ground black pepper
75 g/3 oz Cheddar cheese, grated
melted margarine or butter, for
 greasing

1 Heat the oven to 200C/400F/Gas 6. Brush 6 individual ovenproof dishes with melted margarine, then coat them evenly with 4 tablespoons of the breadcrumbs. Set aside.

2 Heat the oil in a frying-pan, add the onion and garlic, if using, and fry gently for 3-4 minutes until the onion is soft but not coloured. Set aside to cool for about 5 minutes.

3 Cut the avocado in half. Remove the stone, scoop out the flesh into a bowl, then mash with a fork to a purée. Beat in the egg yolks and parsley, then the cooled onion and salt and pepper to taste.

4 Beat the egg whites until standing in stiff peaks, then fold them into the avocado mixture. Pile into the dishes, scatter remaining crumbs on top and bake in the oven for 20 minutes.

5 Sprinkle the top of the rising mixture with the cheese, then return dishes to the oven for a further 15 minutes until they are well risen and golden. Serve at once.

Spaghetti with olives

SERVES 4

400 g/14 oz spaghetti
150 ml/¼ pint olive oil (see Cook's tip)
1 onion, finely chopped
1 green pepper, deseeded and thinly sliced
4 tomatoes, skinned and chopped
salt and freshly ground black pepper
100 g/4 oz black olives, stoned and halved (see Buying guide)
50 g/2 oz Parmesan cheese, grated, to finish

1 Heat the oil in a large frying-pan with a lid. Add the onion, green pepper and tomatoes, with salt and pepper to taste, then cover the pan and cook over moderate heat for 20 minutes, stirring from time to time.

2 Add the olives to the tomato and pepper mixture in the frying-pan and cook gently for 5 minutes.

3 Meanwhile, bring a large saucepan of salted water to the boil and cook the spaghetti for about 10 minutes, until *al dente* (tender yet firm to the bite). Drain well.

4 Add the drained spaghetti to the frying-pan and turn gently to coat evenly with the sauce. Transfer to a warmed serving dish and serve, sprinkled with Parmesan cheese.

Cook's Notes

 TIME
Preparation takes about 15 minutes. Cooking takes 25 minutes.

 COOK'S TIP
It is essential to use olive oil for this dish, to ensure the sauce has the right flavour and a consistency just to coat the spaghetti.

BUYING GUIDE
There are many different varieties of olive, some very large, some very small. They are available pickled in brine in jars, or loose from delicatessens. Choose medium-sized olives for this recipe.

 VARIATION
2 large celery stalks, thinly sliced, could replace the pepper: the flavour of celery combines very well with olives too.

 DID YOU KNOW
Olives grow profusely in Mediterranean countries, especially in France, Italy, Spain and Greece. Black olives, which are fully ripe when picked, are often used in the cooking of these countries. Green olives, which are picked unripe, are most often used for garnishing rather than cooking.

●810 calories/3375 kj per portion

Cheese fondue

SERVES 4

225 g/8 oz Gouda or Gruyère
  cheese, finely grated
225 g/8 oz mature Cheddar cheese,
  finely grated
1 clove garlic (optional)
300 ml/½ pint dry white wine
1 tablespoon plain flour
1 teaspoon kirsch (optional)
pinch of freshly grated nutmeg
salt and freshly ground black pepper

TO SERVE

selection of raw crisp vegetables
  (celery stalks, cauliflower florets,
  carrot sticks)
French bread, cut into cubes

1 Halve garlic, if using and rub cut surfaces on inside of a heavy-based fondue pan or saucepan.
2 Pour the wine into the pan and heat until it starts to boil.
3 Put the flour in a polythene bag, add the cheeses, and shake.
4 Turn the heat to low and slowly add the cheese to the wine, stirring.
5 Add the kirsch, if using, and nutmeg, salt and pepper to taste, then cook for 10-15 minutes on the lowest possible heat to allow the fondue flavours to develop. ⚠
6 To serve: place fondue pan over spirit burner, or pour fondue into warmed individual soup bowls. Serve at once, using forks to dip crisp vegetables and cubes of bread into the fondue.

Cook's Notes

TIME
30-40 minutes, including preparation.

WATCHPOINT
Do not let the mixture become too hot during cooking or the cheese will become stringy.

ECONOMY
This is an inexpensive version of the traditional Swiss cheese fondue which uses equal quantities of Gruyère and Emmental. Mature Cheddar is more economical.

●275 calories/1150 kj per portion

Mixed fruit curry

SERVES 4

1 banana

½ honeydew melon, cut into 2.5 cm/1 inch cubes (see Buying guide)

100 g/4 oz each green and black grapes, halved and deseeded

1 orange, divided into segments

1 red dessert apple, cored (see Cook's tips)

50 g/2 oz creamed coconut, broken into pieces (see Buying guide)

2 tablespoons curry paste (see Cook's tips)

150 ml/¼ pint soured cream

1 Put the coconut, curry paste and soured cream into a large saucepan. Stir over low heat until the mixture is well blended.

2 Peel the banana, cut into 1 cm/½ inch slices and add to pan with the melon, grapes and orange. Cook gently, stirring, for 3-4 min- utes until the fruit is warm. Cut the apple into wedges, stir in and warm through. Spoon into a serving dish and serve at once.

Cook's Notes

TIME
20 minutes preparation, 5-6 minutes cooking.

SERVING IDEAS
Serve hot with plain boiled rice. Alternative- ly, serve for a snack or a part of a buffet party accompanied by salad and cold cooked meats.

BUYING GUIDE
Blocks of creamed coco- nut are available in packets from supermarkets and Indian food shops.

Choose a melon that is not too ripe or it will break up.

VARIATIONS
Add 100 g/4 oz diced cooked chicken, ham or bacon to the fruit mixture for a more substantial meal.

COOK'S TIPS
Use an apple corer to remove the core and leave the skin on to add colour.

Use curry paste for this dish rather than curry powder. As the dish is only cooked for a few minutes, curry powder will give an uncooked flavour to the sauce.

●280 calories/1150 kj per portion

Spaghetti supreme

SERVES 4

**250 g/9 oz wholewheat spaghetti
salt**
1 teaspoon vegetable oil
50 g/2 oz butter
**200 g/7 oz blue Stilton cheese, cut
into small cubes**
**25 g/1 oz walnut pieces, roughly
chopped**
150 ml/¼ pint single cream
freshly ground black pepper
**65 g/2½ oz watercress, trimmed of
thick stalks, finely chopped**

1 Bring a large saucepan of salted water to the boil. Swirl in the oil, then add the spaghetti. Bring back to the boil and simmer for about 20 minutes, until the spaghetti is tender but still firm to the bite.

2 Meanwhile, melt the butter in a small saucepan. Add the Stilton and cook over very low heat, mashing with a wooden spoon, until the cheese has melted. Remove the pan from the heat and then stir in the chopped walnuts. Gradually add the cream, stirring vigorously. Season with a little salt and plenty of pepper. Set aside until just before the spaghetti is ready to serve.

3 Return the sauce to low heat, add the watercress and warm through. [!]

4 Drain the spaghetti and rinse with boiling water. Drain again and transfer to a warmed serving dish. Pour over the sauce and then toss gently until the spaghetti is evenly coated with sauce. Serve the dish at once (see Serving ideas).

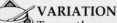

Cook's Notes

TIME
Preparation takes about 30 minutes.

WATCHPOINT
Warm the cheese sauce through gently – it will separate if it becomes too hot. If this does happen, remove pan from heat and beat the sauce with a wooden spoon until it is thick and creamy.

VARIATION
Try other shapes of wholewheat pasta, such as macaroni or shells or tagliatelle.

SERVING IDEAS
Serve with a crisp green or mixed salad, and a bottle of red wine.

● 625 calories/2600 kj per portion

Carrot and nut roast

SERVES 4

250 g/9 oz carrots, coarsely grated
100 g/4 oz cashew nuts or pieces (see Economy)
100 g/4 oz walnut pieces
100 g/4 oz granary or wholewheat bread
50 g/2 oz margarine or butter
1 onion, finely chopped
6 tablespoons hot vegetable stock
2 teaspoons yeast extract
1 teaspoon honey
1 teaspoon dried mixed herbs
2 teaspoons lemon juice
salt and freshly ground black pepper
margarine or butter, for greasing

1 Heat the oven to 180C/350F/Gas 4. Grease an 850 ml/1½ pint shallow ovenproof dish. Grind the cashews, walnuts and bread together in batches in a blender until they are fairly fine. Tip them into a bowl.
2 Melt the margarine in a saucepan, add the onion and fry gently for 5 minutes until soft and lightly coloured. Add the carrots and cook, stirring, for a further 5 minutes. Remove from the pan with a slotted spoon and add to the nuts and bread in the bowl.
3 Put the hot stock in a bowl, add the yeast extract and honey and stir until dissolved. Stir into the nut mixture with the herbs and lemon juice. Taste the mixture and season with salt and pepper. ⚠
4 Spoon mixture into prepared dish and bake in the oven for 45 minutes. Serve hot or cold (see Serving ideas).

Cook's Notes

 TIME
35 minutes preparation and 45 minutes baking.

 SERVING IDEAS
Serve hot with baked potatoes, sliced tomatoes and a green vegetable or salad or serve cold with mixed salads. This carrot and nut roast is best served straight from the dish. It can be cut into thick slices or wedges depending on the shape of the dish that is being used.

 ECONOMY
Some health food shops and supermarkets sell broken nuts which are less expensive than whole nuts.

 WATCHPOINT
Taste the mixture before adding any salt, particularly if using salted nuts.

 COOK'S TIP
This dish can be made ahead and then reheated in a 180C/350F/Gas 4 oven for about 30 minutes.

 VARIATION
Use any combination of nuts in this dish, as long as their total weight is the same as the nuts used here.

● 450 calories/1875 kj per portion

Pasta kugel

SERVES 4

200 g/7 oz wholewheat pasta rings
3 eggs
225 g/8 oz curd cheese
150 ml/¼ pint soured cream
2 tablespoons soft brown sugar
100 g/4 oz seedless raisins
¼ teaspoon salt
¼ teaspoon ground cinnamon
¼ teaspoon freshly grated nutmeg
margarine, for greasing

TOPPING
2 tablespoons chopped mixed nuts
¼ teaspoon ground cinnamon
15 g/½ oz butter

1 Heat the oven to 180C/350F/Gas 4. Grease a 1 L/2 pint ovenproof dish generously with margarine.
2 Bring a pan of salted water to the boil and cook the pasta rings for

12 minutes or according to packet instructions until they are cooked but still firm to the bite.
3 Meanwhile, beat the eggs in a bowl, add the curd cheese, soured cream and sugar and beat with a fork until smooth. Mix in the raisins, salt and spices.
4 Drain the cooked pasta rings and return them to the rinsed-out pan. Pour the curd cheese mixture over

the pasta and stir it until evenly coated. Transfer the mixture to the prepared dish, sprinkle with nuts and cinnamon and dot the surface with the butter.
5 Bake in the oven, uncovered, for about 30 minutes, until the top is golden and filling has set around the edge but is still creamy in the middle. Serve at once straight from the dish (see Serving ideas).

Cook's Notes

 TIME
20 minutes preparation and about 30 minutes baking in the oven.

? DID YOU KNOW
Kugel is the Jewish name for a pudding, usually made of noodles or potatoes and baked. Although many kugels, like this one, are semi-sweet, they are not meant to be served as desserts.

 SERVING IDEAS
This wholewheat pasta kugel makes a tasty brunch, lunch or supper dish, served with green salad or fruit, such as sliced pears or peaches.

 VARIATION
Other pasta shapes can be used instead of rings, such as shells or wheels.

●535 calories/2250 kj per portion

Supper eggs

SERVES 4

750 g/1½ lb potatoes, cut into large chunks (see Buying guide)
4 eggs (see Buying guide)
25 g/1 oz butter
1 Spanish onion, chopped
1 tablespoon milk
75 g/3 oz Cheddar cheese, grated
salt and freshly ground black pepper
50 g/2 oz Double Gloucester cheese, grated

1 Put potatoes in a large saucepan, cover them with cold water and bring to the boil. Simmer gently for about 20 minutes until tender.

2 Meanwhile, melt the butter in a frying-pan, add the onion and fry for 5 minutes until the onion is soft and lightly browned.

3 Drain the potatoes well, then return to the saucepan and mash with the milk until smooth. Stir in the onion and butter mixture and the Cheddar cheese. Season this mixture to taste with salt and freshly ground black pepper.

4 Heat the grill to medium.

5 Spoon the potato mixture into a shallow flameproof dish. Fluff up the surface of the potato with a fork. Using the back of a spoon, make 4 shallow depressions in potato, about 7.5 cm/3 inches wide and no more than 1 cm/½ inch deep.

6 Break an egg into each hollow and place the dish under the grill for 7-10 minutes, until the eggs are just barely set.

7 Remove dish and allow eggs to cool for 2 minutes (see Cook's tip). Sprinkle with Double Gloucester cheese and serve at once.

Cook's Notes

TIME
Preparation takes about 30 minutes. Cooking the eggs takes 9-12 minutes.

VARIATION
Put a layer of sliced skinned tomatoes in the base of the dish before putting the mashed potato on top.

COOK'S TIP
Allowing the eggs to stand before serving helps the egg white to firm and set completely (it continues to cook by retained heat) without the yolks becoming overcooked and tough.

●405 calories/1700 kj per portion

BUYING GUIDE
Use old floury, potatoes like King Edwards or Desirées for the best results.

For this dish, try to make sure the eggs are as fresh as possible. They will taste much better and the egg white will be thicker and less inclined to run out of the potato hollows.

Savoury celery supper

SERVES 4

1 head celery, cut into 2.5 cm/1 inch
    lengths
salt
2 tablespoons capers
2 tablespoons finely chopped fresh
    parsley
1 large gherkin, finely chopped
2 large potatoes, cooked and sliced
3 hard-boiled eggs, sliced
150 g/5 oz mature Cheddar cheese,
    grated
25 g/1 oz plain flour
2 × 150 g/5 oz cartons natural
    yoghurt
2 eggs, beaten
freshly ground black pepper
1 packet potato crisps, crushed
margarine, for greasing

1 Heat the oven to 190C/375F/Gas 5. Grease a 2 L/3½ pint ovenproof dish.

2 Bring a pan of salted water to the boil and cook the celery for 5-10 minutes until just tender.

3 Meanwhile, mix the capers, parsley and gherkin in a small bowl.

4 Drain the celery thoroughly and arrange half in the prepared dish. Cover with layers of half the potato slices, half the egg slices and 100 g/ 4 oz cheese, sprinkling half the caper, parsley and gherkin mixture between the layers. Repeat with the remaining ingredients, but reverse the order of the layers: egg, potato and celery sprinkling them with the remaining caper mixture.

5 In a bowl, blend the flour with a little of the yoghurt, then gradually whisk in the remainder. Mix in the beaten eggs, then season with salt and pepper to taste and pour into the dish.

6 Mix the reserved cheese with the crushed crisps and sprinkle over the surface. Bake in the oven for about 30 minutes.

7 Just before the end of the cooking time, heat the grill to high. When the mixture is cooked and the custard set, place the dish under the grill for about 5 minutes, or until the top is brown and crisp. Serve hot, straight from the dish.

Cheesy vegetable curry

SERVES 4

150 g/5 oz mature Cheddar cheese, cut into 1 cm/½ inch cubes
40 g/1½ oz margarine or butter
1 large onion, chopped
1 small green pepper, deseeded and cut into strips
2 small carrots, halved lengthways and thinly sliced
4 small or 2 large courgettes, halved lengthways and cut into 1 cm/ ½ inch slices
1 large cooking apple, peeled, cored and cut into 2 cm/¾ inch dice
2 teaspoons curry powder
40 g/1½ oz plain flour
600 ml/1 pint chicken stock
25 g/1 oz sultanas
salt
2 tablespoons mango chutney, chopped

Cook's Notes

TIME
This superquick curry takes only 15 minutes preparation, and 15 minutes to cook.

VARIATION
Instead of cheese, use diced cooked meat, but add with the sultanas in stage 2.

SERVING IDEAS
Serve each portion of curry in a ring of boiled or savoury rice.

Offer a tomato salad with a mint and yoghurt dressing as an accompaniment, and for those who like their curries really hot, serve lime pickle as an additional side dish.

WATCHPOINT
The cheese cubes must not be added to the vegetables and sauce until the very last moment or they will melt into the sauce.

●365 calories/1525 kj per portion

1 Melt the margarine in a saucepan, add the onion, green pepper and carrots and fry gently for 3-4 minutes, stirring, until the onions are soft but not coloured. Add the courgettes, apple and curry powder and cook for 2 minutes, stirring.
2 Sprinkle in the flour, cook for 1-2 minutes, stirring, then gradually blend in the stock. Bring to the boil, stirring, then add the sultanas and salt to taste. Lower the heat, cover the pan and simmer for 5 minutes.
3 Add the mango chutney, then stir in the cubed cheese.⚠ Serve at once in an attractive bowl.

Stilton quiche

SERVES 4-6

150-175 g/6 oz shortcrust pastry,
   defrosted if frozen
100 g/4 oz Stilton cheese, grated
150 ml/¼ pint milk
150 ml/¼ pint double cream
3 large eggs
2 tablespoons chopped parsley
25 g/1 oz Stilton cheese, crumbled,
   to garnish (optional)

1 Heat the oven to 200C/400F/Gas 6.
2 Roll out the pastry on a floured surface and use to line a 20 cm/8 inch flan ring placed on a baking sheet. Refrigerate for 30 minutes.
3 Put 100 g/4 oz grated Stilton, the milk, cream, eggs and parsley in a bowl and whisk together, using a fork, until well blended. Pour the mixture into the prepared flan ring and bake in the oven for 40-45 minutes, until the filling has set.
4 Carefully remove the flan ring and transfer the quiche to a serving dish. Serve hot or cold, garnished with crumbled cheese if liked.

Egg and avocado mayonnaise

SERVES 4
6 small eggs
2 small avocados
75 g/3 oz full-fat soft cheese
2 tablespoons thick bottled
    mayonnaise
1 teaspoon lemon juice
¼ teaspoon Worcestershire sauce
salt and freshly ground black pepper
bunch of watercress, washed
1 tablespoon chopped fresh parsley
thin slices of brown bread and
    butter, to serve

1 Place the eggs in a small sauce-pan. Cover with cold water. Bring to the boil, then boil gently for 8 minutes. Drain and rinse under cold running water, until cool. !
2 Meanwhile, cut the avocados in half lengthways, scoop out the flesh and put it into a bowl. Mash with a

fork and then beat in the cheese followed by the mayonnaise. ! Stir in lemon juice and Worcestershire sauce and season to taste with salt and pepper (see Cook's tip).
3 Shell the eggs then cut in half

lengthways. Place 3 halves, cut side down, on beds of watercress on each of 4 small plates. Spoon the avocado mayonnaise over the eggs.
4 Sprinkle with parsley and serve with brown bread and butter.

Cook's Notes

 TIME
Hard-boiling eggs and making mayonnaise will take 20 minutes.

 COOK'S TIP
If a very smooth-textured mayonnaise is preferred, work the ingredients in a blender or food processor.

 SERVING IDEAS
This is a surprisingly filling supper dish but for a more substantial meal, allow 2 eggs per person and serve with bowls of watercress, chopped chicory and celery.

! WATCHPOINTS
It is important not to overcook hard-boiled eggs, otherwise they develop an unpleasant rubbery texture and become indigestible. Eight to 11 minutes, depending on size, is the maximum suggested time. Rinsing in cold water is essential to ensure that the heat stored in the shell does not continue cooking the interior of the hard-boiled egg.

The mayonnaise should be used at once or the avocado flesh will discolour.

●390 calories/1625 kj per portion

Carrot and potato soufflé

SERVES 4

500 g/1 lb carrots, cut into 2.5 cm/
   1 inch pieces
350 g/12 oz potatoes, cut into
   2.5 cm/1 inch pieces
salt
25 g/1 oz margarine or butter
2 tablespoons milk
4-5 teaspoons French mustard
100 g/4 oz mature Cheddar cheese,
   finely grated
5 eggs, separated
freshly ground black pepper
margarine, for greasing

1 Bring the carrots to the boil in a large saucepan of salted water, lower the heat and cook for about 15 minutes or until tender.

2 Meanwhile, in a separate saucepan, cook the potatoes in the same way for about 10 minutes or until tender.

3 Heat the oven to 200C/400F/Gas 6. Grease a 1.5 L/2½ pint soufflé dish.

4 Drain the cooked vegetables and transfer to a clean saucepan. Mash with the margarine and milk until smooth. Transfer to a large bowl (see Cook's tip) and mix in the mustard, cheese, egg yolks and salt and pepper to taste. Beat with a wooden spoon until smooth.

5 In a clean, dry bowl, whisk the egg whites until stiff but not dry. Using a large metal spoon, fold them lightly into the carrot and potato mixture. Pour into the prepared dish and bake in the oven for 35 minutes, or until the soufflé is well-risen and golden. When lightly shaken, it should only wobble very slightly. Serve at once, straight from the soufflé dish.

98

Vegetable terrine

SERVES 4

12 cabbage leaves (see Buying guide), central midribs removed
salt
1 carrot (weight about 100 g/4 oz), cut into matchstick lengths
1 courgette (weight about 100 g/4 oz), cut into matchstick lengths
200 g/7 oz can sweetcorn and pimiento, drained
2 eggs, plus 1 egg yolk
150 ml/¼ pint milk
3 tablespoons double cream
¼ nutmeg, grated
freshly ground black pepper
vegetable oil, for brushing

TOMATO SAUCE
250 g/9 oz tomatoes, roughly chopped
3 tablespoons natural yoghurt
1 teaspoon French mustard
1 teaspoon Worcestershire sauce
1 teaspoon tomato ketchup
pinch of caster sugar

1 Heat the oven to 170C/325F/Gas 3.
2 Bring a saucepan of salted water to the boil and blanch the cabbage leaves for 2 minutes. Drain and dry on a clean tea-towel.
3 Bring a saucepan of salted water to the boil and put the carrot and courgette matchsticks in to simmer for 5 minutes. Drain and refresh under cold water, drain again.
4 Brush a 1 kg/2 lb loaf tin with vegetable oil. Line the loaf tin with 3 or 4 of the largest cabbage leaves and chop the remainder fairly finely.
5 Put half the carrot and courgette mixture into the lined loaf tin, add half the sweetcorn and pimiento, then half the chopped cabbage. Repeat the layering to make 6 layers in all.
6 Whisk the eggs lightly with the extra yolk, milk, cream and nutmeg. Season with salt and pepper. Carefully pour the egg mixture into the loaf tin, gently easing the vegetables apart in several places with a round-bladed knife, to make sure the egg mixture is evenly distributed through the tin and goes right to the bottom. Fold any protruding cabbage leaves over the filling. Cover the tin with foil.
7 Set the loaf tin in a roasting tin. Pour in hot water to come three-quarters up the sides of the loaf tin and cook for 1½-2 hours, until the custard is set and firm to the touch. Remove the loaf tin from the roasting tin and cool. Chill overnight in the refrigerator.
8 To make the sauce: put the tomatoes in a blender for a few seconds until liquidized, then sieve to remove the skins and seeds.
9 Mix the tomato purée with the remaining sauce ingredients, stirring to make sure they are well combined. Season to taste with salt and pepper. Cover with cling film and chill for at least 2 hours.
10 To serve: allow the terrine to stand at room temperature for about 10 minutes. Run a knife round the sides of the terrine, invert a serving plate on top and shake gently to unmould. Serve cut in slices (see Cook's tips) with the tomato sauce.

Maytime flan

SERVES 4

215 g/7½ oz frozen shortcrust pastry, defrosted

FILLING
225 g/8 oz cottage cheese with chives
3 eggs
25 g/1 oz butter
100 g/4 oz button mushrooms, sliced
½ teaspoon dried thyme
salt and freshly ground black pepper
1 tomato, thinly sliced

1 Heat the oven to 200C/400F/Gas 6.
2 Roll out the pastry on a lightly floured surface and use to line an 18 cm/7 inch loose-bottomed flan tin or flan ring standing on a baking sheet. Prick the pastry with a fork, line with greaseproof paper and fill with baking beans. Bake blind in the oven for 10 minutes.
3 Meanwhile, make the filling: put the cottage cheese into a bowl with the eggs and beat together with a fork until well mixed.
4 Melt the butter in a small saucepan, add the mushrooms and fry gently for 2 minutes, stirring. Drain well, then add the mushrooms to the cottage cheese mixture. Stir in the thyme and season to taste with salt and pepper.
5 Remove the greaseproof paper and beans from the pastry case, pour in the cottage cheese mixture and arrange the tomato slices around the edge. Return to the oven and bake for 35 minutes until the filling is golden brown and set.
6 Leave to stand for 5-10 minutes. Remove sides of tin and place the flan on a serving plate. Serve while still warm or leave until cold.

Cook's Notes

TIME
Preparation and cooking take 50-55 minutes.

SERVING IDEAS
Serve the flan with white wine and salad.

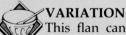
VARIATION
This flan can be made with homemade wholemeal pastry. Use half wholemeal flour and half plain flour, if wished.

● 385 calories/1625 kj per portion

Sunshine supper

SERVES 4

1 large aubergine
salt
4 tablespoons olive oil
1 clove garlic, crushed (optional)
1 onion, chopped
1 green pepper, deseeded and finely chopped
400 g/14 oz can tomatoes, chopped (see Economy)
75 ml/3 fl oz red wine
2 teaspoons tomato purée
½ teaspoon sugar
1 teaspoon dried basil
freshly ground black pepper
100 g/4 oz ribbon noodles (see Buying guide)
6 slices processed cheese
25 g/1 oz Parmesan cheese, grated
melted butter, for greasing

1 Wipe the aubergine with a damp cloth and trim off the stalk. Slice the aubergine into 5 mm/¼ inch thick slices and put them in a colander in layers, sprinkling salt between each layer. Cover with a plate and place a heavy weight on top. Leave for about 1 hour to draw out the bitter juices then rinse the slices and pat dry on absorbent paper.

2 Heat the oven to 180C/350F/Gas 4.

3 Heat 1 tablespoon of the oil in a saucepan, add the garlic, if using, the onion and green pepper and fry gently for about 5 minutes until the onion is soft and lightly coloured. Stir in tomatoes with juices, wine and tomato purée. Bring to boil, stir in the sugar and basil and season with salt and pepper to taste. Let the sauce boil gently to reduce and thicken.

4 Meanwhile, bring a pan of salted water to the boil and add 1 teaspoon of oil. Cook the noodles for 10-12 minutes until just tender then drain thoroughly.

5 Heat the remaining oil in a frying-pan, add the aubergine slices and fry gently until they are lightly coloured on both sides. Remove with a slotted spoon and drain on absorbent paper.

6 Grease an ovenproof dish with melted butter and spread a third of the tomato sauce over the bottom.

Put half the noodles on top, followed by half the aubergine slices and half the processed cheese. Cover with another third of the tomato sauce and then the remaining noodles, aubergine slices and processed cheese. Spread the remaining tomato sauce over the cheese slices and sprinkle the Parmesan cheese on top.

7 Cook in the oven for about 20 minutes, until heated through. Serve immediately straight from the dish.

Cook's Notes

TIME
Draining the aubergines takes 1 hour; allow another 20-25 minutes for the rest of the preparation. Cooking takes 20 minutes.

BUYING GUIDE
Look for green noodles available in most supermarkets; they are particularly suitable for this dish.

●355 calories/1500 kj per portion

SERVING IDEAS
This delicious supper dish needs only a salad accompaniment to make it a complete meal.

ECONOMY
Use fresh tomatoes for the sauce when they are plentiful and low in price—you will need 350 g/12 oz. Skin and chop them and add to the onion and green pepper with a little extra wine.

Egg and onion bake

SERVES 4

4 eggs
2 large onions, finely chopped
salt and freshly ground black pepper
600 ml/1 pint hot milk (see
   Cook's tip)
75 g/3 oz Cheddar cheese, grated
15 g/½ oz margarine or butter
1 tablespoon vegetable oil
2 tablespoons chopped fresh chervil
   (see Variation)
margarine, for greasing

SAUCE

25 g/1 oz margarine or butter
25 g/1 oz plain flour
300 ml/½ pint milk
100 g/4 oz Cheddar cheese, grated

1 Heat the oven to 150C/300F/Gas 2
and grease a 1.25 L/2 pint ovenproof
dish with margarine.

2 Put the eggs in a bowl and season
with salt and pepper. Whisk the
eggs, then whisk in the milk and
cheese and pour into the prepared
dish. Half-fill a roasting tin with
boiling water and place the dish in
the tin. Bake in the oven for 1½
hours or until the mixture is firm.
3 About 15 minutes before the end
of the cooking time, heat the
margarine and oil in a frying-pan.
Add the onions and fry gently for 5
minutes until soft and lightly
coloured. Stir in the chervil and
remove from the heat.
4 Heat the grill to high.
5 Meanwhile, make the sauce: melt
the margarine in a small saucepan,
sprinkle in the flour and stir over
low heat for 1-2 minutes until straw-
coloured. Remove from the heat and
gradually stir in the milk. Return to
the heat and simmer, stirring, until
thick and smooth. Stir in half the
grated cheese and season to taste
with salt and pepper.
6 When the egg mixture is cooked,
spoon the onion mixture over top.

7 Spoon the sauce over onions and
sprinkle with the remaining cheese.
8 Place the dish under the grill until
the cheese has melted and is golden
brown and bubbling. Serve at once.

Cook's Notes

TIME
Preparing and cooking
this dish take about
1 hour 35 minutes.

SERVING IDEAS
Serve with chips and a
tossed green salad.

VARIATION
If chervil is unavailable,
use parsley instead.

COOK'S TIP
The hot milk speeds up
the cooking process as it
starts to set the egg yolks.

● 540 calories/2275 kj per portion

Nutty rissoles

MAKES 12

225 g/8 oz mixed nuts, finely
    chopped (see Buying guide)
25 g/1 oz butter
175 g/6 oz onions, finely chopped
1 large clove garlic, crushed
    (optional)
175 g/6 oz mushrooms, finely
    chopped
100 g/4 oz fresh wholemeal
    breadcrumbs
1 tablespoon finely chopped fresh
    parsley
2 teaspoons dried mixed herbs
2 tablespoons tomato purée
1 teaspoon soy sauce
1 egg, beaten
salt and freshly ground black pepper
3-4 tablespoons plain flour, for
    coating
a little vegetable oil, for frying
mushroom slices and walnut
    halves, to garnish

1 Melt the butter in a saucepan then add the onions and garlic, if using, and fry over gentle heat for 4-5 minutes until soft.
2 Remove the pan from the heat and stir in the nuts, mushrooms, breadcrumbs, parsley and mixed herbs until well blended. Add the tomato purée and soy sauce and sufficient beaten egg to bind the mixture together. Season to taste with salt and pepper.
3 Roll heaped tablespoons of the mixture in flour to form 12 balls then flatten them into rissoles about 7.5 cm/3 inches in diameter.
4 Arrange the prepared rissoles on a floured baking sheet and leave in the refrigerator or in a cold place for about 1 hour.
5 Heat the oven to 110C/225F/Gas ¼.
6 Heat a little vegetable oil in a large frying-pan and fry the rissoles in 2 batches, cooking them for 3-5 minutes on each side or until crisp and golden brown. Remove with slotted spoon; drain on absorbent paper. Put them in the oven to keep warm while cooking the remaining rissoles. When all the rissoles are cooked, garnish with mushroom slices and walnut halves and serve them at once, while still piping hot.

Herby beans with eggs

SERVES 4

225 g/8 oz fresh or frozen sliced French or runner beans (see Cook's tip)
225 g/8 oz fresh or frozen broad beans
225 g/8 oz fresh or frozen peas
salt
4 large eggs, hard-boiled and quartered

SAUCE

25 g/1 oz margarine or butter
25 g/1 oz plain flour
425 ml/¾ pint milk
2 tablespoons chopped fresh parsley
2 tablespoons chopped fresh tarragon or 1½ teaspoons dried tarragon
2 teaspoons lemon juice
freshly ground black pepper

1 Heat the oven to 110C/225F/Gas ¼. Bring a large saucepan of salted water to the boil. Add the fresh or frozen vegetables and cook for 10-15 minutes until just tender.

2 Meanwhile, make the sauce: melt the margarine in a small saucepan, sprinkle in the flour and stir over low heat for 1-2 minutes until straw-coloured. Remove from the heat and gradually stir in the milk. Add the parsley and tarragon, return to the heat and simmer, stirring, until thickened and smooth. Stir in the lemon juice, and season to taste with salt and pepper.

3 Drain the vegetables. Reserve one-third of the sauce and mix the rest into the vegetables. Heat through, very gently, transfer to a warmed serving dish and keep warm in the oven.

4 Heat the remaining sauce in the same pan. When it is very hot but not boiling, arrange the eggs on the vegetables and drizzle the hot sauce over them. Serve at once straight from the dish.

Tomato, cheese and basil flan

SERVES 4

150-175 g/6 oz shortcrust pastry,
  defrosted if frozen
4 large tomatoes (about 250 g/9 oz),
  sliced
300 ml/½ pint milk
3 large eggs
1½ teaspoons dried basil (see Did
  you know)
75 g/3 oz mature Cheddar cheese,
  grated
salt and freshly ground black pepper
a few tomato slices, to garnish
  (optional)

1 Heat the oven to 190C/375F/Gas 5.
2 Roll out the shortcrust pastry on a floured surface and use to line a 20 cm/8 inch plain flan ring set on a baking sheet.
3 Arrange the 250 g/9 oz tomato slices overlapping in the flan case. In a bowl, whisk together the milk, eggs, basil, 50 g/2 oz of the cheese and salt and pepper to taste.
4 Pour the mixture into the flan case and sprinkle over the remaining cheese. Bake in the oven for 40-45 minutes until the filling is set and golden brown on top.
5 Allow the flan to cool for 5 minutes, then carefully remove the flan ring. Transfer the flan to a serving dish, then garnish with tomato slices, if liked.

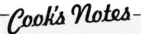

Cook's Notes

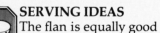

TIME
Preparation takes about 20 minutes, baking 40-45 minutes.

DID YOU KNOW
The flavour of sweet basil perfectly complements tomato, and this is a classic combination in many dishes, particularly those of Italian origin.

Fresh herbs are always preferable in cooking, but fresh basil is not readily available, though it can sometimes be found in specialist greengrocers during the summer months.

Remember, if you want to grow basil, that it is an annual and so you will need to buy a new plant each year. It likes a sunny, sheltered spot.

There are two main kinds, with which you can experiment. Sweet basil has largish, shiny dark green leaves and white flowers. Bush basil has many small pale green leaves and tiny white flowers. Bush and sweet basil have an equally good flavour.

The strong, aromatic flavour of basil is delicious in egg, mushroom and pasta dishes, as well as with tomatoes.

SERVING IDEAS
The flan is equally good served warm or cold. If serving as a main course for lunch or supper, accompany it with a green salad or a salad of lightly cooked French beans tossed in oil and vinegar and garnished with some lightly toasted almonds.

This tasty flan makes perfect picnic food. It would also serve 6-8 as an appetizing starter for either a lunch or supper party. Try accompanying it with a spicy tomato relish.

●385 calories/1600 kj per portion

Spanish vegetable omelette

SERVES 4

500 g/1 lb potatoes, cut into 1 cm/½ inch dice (see Cook's tip)
salt
175 g/6 oz fresh French beans or 100 g/4 oz frozen French beans
2 tablespoons vegetable oil
1 onion, chopped
1 red pepper, deseeded and diced
7 eggs, beaten
2 tablespoons finely chopped fresh parsley
½ teaspoon sweet paprika
freshly ground black pepper
a little extra finely chopped fresh parsley, to garnish

1 Bring a pan of salted water to the boil and cook the potatoes for about 5 minutes, until just tender but not mushy. Drain, refresh in cold water and drain again. Put the potatoes in a large bowl.

2 If using fresh beans, bring a pan of salted water to the boil and cook them for about 8 minutes until tender but still crisp. If using frozen beans, cook for about 5 minutes. Drain, refresh in cold water and drain again. Cut the beans into 2.5-4 cm/1-1½ inch lengths and add to the potatoes in the bowl.

3 Heat the oil in a large non-stick frying-pan, add the onion and red pepper and cook gently for about 5 minutes, stirring occasionally, until softened but not coloured. Remove the onion and pepper from the pan with a slotted spoon, draining all the oil back into the pan, and add to the potatoes and beans.

4 Add the beaten eggs, parsley and sweet paprika to the vegetables in the bowl and stir lightly together. Season to taste with salt and pepper.

5 Reheat the oil in the pan over low heat and pour in the omelette mixture. Level out the vegetables and leave to cook very gently for 15-20 minutes, until the bottom is set but the top is still creamy. Meanwhile, heat the grill to high.

6 Set the frying-pan under the grill at the lowest position from the heat for 2-3 minutes, until the top of the omelette is set and light golden. Loosen the omelette from the pan with a palette knife, then with a fish slice slide it carefully on to a large plate. Sprinkle lightly with chopped parsley and leave to cool slightly. Serve the omelette cut into wedges.

Cook's Notes

TIME
Preparation and cooking take about 1 hour.

SERVING IDEAS
Serve the omelette warm or cold, on its own for a snack, or with French bread and salad for a lunch or supper dish. Alternatively, try slipping wedges of the hot omelette into lightly toasted pitta bread pockets, adding slices of cucumber or tomato.

VARIATIONS
Use peas or broad beans instead of French beans, or replace half the potato with diced carrot. Use 8 spring onions, trimmed and cut into 5 mm/¼ inch slices, in place of ordinary onion, and finely chopped fresh mint makes a refreshing alternative to parsley. Add 50 g/2 oz left-over cooked chicken, ham or sausage, finely chopped, to the recipe for extra flavour and nourishment.

COOK'S TIP
If you want to use up left-over potatoes in this recipe, you will need about 350 g/12 oz cooked potatoes.

●315 calories/1325 kj per portion

106

Quick and easy homemade pasta

SERVES 2

225 g/8 oz plain flour
salt
75-100 ml/3-3½ fl oz cold water

1 Sift the flour and ¼ teaspoon salt into the goblet of a blender or food processor. Work for a few seconds, gradually adding the water until a dough is formed which has the consistency of fine breadcrumbs, but forms into a ball when it is pressed together (see Variations).

2 Remove the dough, press it into a ball, then place on a lightly floured surface and cut the dough into two equal halves.

3 Roll out 1 piece of dough very thinly so that the board can just be seen through the dough – it should measure 30 × 25 cm/12 × 10 inches. Trim off any dry edges of the dough with a sharp knife.

4 Fold and cut the dough to make long narrow ribbons (see Variations). Let pasta dry for 2-3 minutes while rolling, folding and cutting second piece of dough. Allow this batch of the pasta to dry for 2-3 minutes before cooking.

5 Bring a large pan of well salted water to boil and plunge all the pasta into it. Bring back to the boil and cook for 30 seconds. Drain and serve at once. Serve with your favourite pasta sauce, or buttered and then sprinkled with freshly grated Parmesan cheese and freshly ground black pepper.

Cook's Notes

TIME
The pasta takes only 15 minutes to make; cooking it takes about 1 minute.

! WATCHPOINT
Add the water slowly when making the pasta, as it is important not to get the dough too wet.

✳ FREEZING
Fresh pasta freezes well: do not pull the ribbons apart after cutting dough. Wrap cut 'sausage' in foil, seal, label and freeze for 2-3 months. To serve: thaw overnight in refrigerator or cook straight from frozen for an additional 2 minutes, stirring constantly to pull the dough ribbons apart as they soften.

COOK'S TIP
If you wish to make pasta for 4, double the quantities here, then cut dough into 4 pieces, as large quantities of pasta dry out and become difficult to handle.

VARIATIONS
When making dough, add an egg for a tastier pasta. Or, to make pretty green pasta, add a drop of green food colouring to the water.

Cut the dough into very thin ribbons. These are ideal for serving in soup and are a great favourite with children.

● 400 calories/1675 kj per portion

Dutch fondue

SERVES 4

250 g/9 oz flat mushrooms with
 their stalks, finely chopped
600 ml/1 pint chicken stock
4 tablespoons cornflour
150 ml/¼ pint milk
250 g/9 oz Gouda cheese, finely
 grated (see Variations)
1 tablespoon finely chopped fresh
 parsley
1 teaspoon Worcestershire sauce
salt and freshly ground black pepper
mushroom slices, to garnish

TO SERVE

1 small French loaf, cut into 2.5 cm/
 1 inch cubes
500 g/1 lb pork sausages, fried and
 thickly sliced

1 Put the chopped mushrooms in a
saucepan with the stock and bring
to the boil. Lower the heat, cover
and simmer gently for 10 minutes.

2 In a small bowl, blend the
cornflour to a smooth paste with a
little of the milk. Stir into the
mushroom stock, then add the
remaining milk. Bring to the boil,
lower the heat and simmer for 2
minutes, stirring all the time.

3 Turn the heat under the pan to the
lowest setting. Add the grated
cheese to the pan, 2 tablespoons at a
time, stirring well until all the

cheese has melted. Do not allow the
mixture to simmer. !

4 Remove the pan from the heat and
stir in the fresh parsley and
Worcestershire sauce, with salt and
pepper to taste. Pour the fondue
into a warmed serving bowl, ! or 4
individual bowls, garnish with
mushroom slices and serve at once.
Hand the bread cubes and sliced
fried sausages separately (see Variations). Provide forks for dipping.

TIME
Preparation and cooking
take 40 minutes.

VARIATIONS
Add 50 g/2 oz finely
grated mature Cheddar
cheese with the Gouda, and stir
1 tablespoon dry sherry into the
fondue just before serving.

Lightly steamed still crunchy
broccoli spears or cauliflower
florets may be used for dipping.

WATCHPOINTS
It is vital not to allow the
mixture to simmer (no
sign of a bubble should appear
on the surface) or the fondue
will become stringy and
separate and will not look as nice.

Make sure that the serving
bowl or bowls are well heated,
or the fondue will cool and
thicken around the edges.

●665 calories/2800 kj per portion

Egg and spinach nests

SERVES 4

**250 g/9 oz spinach, stalks and large
  midribs removed, shredded**
25 g/1 oz margarine or butter
salt and freshly ground black pepper
4 eggs
4 tablespoons double cream
cayenne, to garnish
margarine, for greasing

1 Heat the oven to 190C/375F/Gas 5.
Grease 4 individual ovenproof
dishes or ramekins.
2 Melt the margarine in a saucepan,
add the spinach and cook gently for
8 minutes, or until soft. Season to
taste with salt and pepper.
3 Divide the spinach between the
prepared dishes. Break 1 egg into
each dish on top of the cooked
spinach mixture.
4 Place the dishes on a baking sheet
and bake in oven for 10 minutes,
until the egg whites begin to set.
Remove from the oven and spoon
1 tablespoon cream over each egg.
Return to the oven and cook for a
further 5 minutes. Sprinkle a little
cayenne over each egg and serve at
once (see Serving ideas).

Cook's Notes

TIME
Preparation 20 minutes,
cooking 15 minutes.

SERVING IDEAS
Serve with wholemeal
toast for a light lunch or
supper. Or serve as a first
course for a dinner party.

DID YOU KNOW
In France the nests are
served in cocotte dishes
– small dishes with a handle.
Cocotte dishes hold one egg.

VARIATIONS
Place 4 tablespoons
chopped cooked
mushrooms or asparagus in the
dish in place of the spinach.

●195 calories/825 kj per portion

Golden vegetable stew

SERVES 4

500 g/1 lb pumpkin, peeled,
   deseeded and cut into
   2 cm/¾ inch cubes
3 tablespoons vegetable oil
1 onion, chopped
250 g/9 oz carrots, thinly sliced
100 g/4 oz red lentils
400 g/14 oz can tomatoes
300 ml/½ pint vegetable stock
½ teaspoon ground mace
salt and freshly ground black pepper

Cook's Notes

TIME
10 minutes to prepare and then 30 minutes cooking time.

SERVING IDEAS
This vegetarian stew is a warming and nourishing supper dish. Top each serving with a dollop of soured cream, if wished, and accompany with warmed crusty brown bread rolls.

●215 calories/900 kj per portion

VARIATIONS
A 200 g/7 oz can sweetcorn, drained, is a tasty addition to this stew. Or, for a lighter dish, omit the soured cream and add the juice of ½ lemon and some chopped fresh parsley.

DID YOU KNOW
Pumpkins, believed to be one of the oldest of cultivated vegetables, provide the mineral calcium as well as vitamins A and C.

1 Heat the oil in a saucepan and fry onion and carrots over moderate heat for 5 minutes.
2 Add the lentils, tomatoes with their juice, stock and mace, and season with salt and pepper to taste. Bring to the boil, lower the heat, cover the pan and simmer gently for 15 minutes.
3 Add the pumpkin to the pan, cover and then simmer gently for a further 15 minutes.
4 Taste and adjust the seasoning if necessary. Serve the stew piping hot, in warmed individual bowls.

Egg and vegetable flan

SERVES 4

150-175 g/5-6 oz shortcrust pastry, defrosted if frozen

FILLING

40 g/1½ oz margarine or butter

100 g/4 oz button mushrooms (see Cook's tips), sliced

25 g/1 oz plain flour

½ teaspoon curry powder

300 ml/½ pint milk

4 hard-boiled eggs, shelled and neatly chopped

100 g/4 oz frozen peas, cooked

salt and freshly ground black pepper

1 Heat the oven to 200C/400F/Gas 6.

2 Roll out the pastry on a lightly floured surface and use it to line an 18 cm/7 inch flan tin. Trim the edges and prick the base in several places with a fork. Place a circle of greaseproof paper or foil in the pastry case and weight it down with a thick even layer of baking beans. Bake for 10 minutes.

3 Remove the greaseproof paper and beans, then return the pastry case to the oven. Bake for a further 10-15 minutes, or until the pastry is crisp and lightly golden.

4 Meanwhile, make the filling: melt the margarine in a saucepan and cook the mushrooms for 2-3 minutes, stirring occasionally. Remove from the pan with a slotted spoon, draining all the margarine back into the pan.

5 Sprinkle the flour and curry powder into pan. Stir over low heat for 1-2 minutes. Remove from the heat and gradually stir in the milk. Return to the heat and simmer, stirring, until thick and smooth.

6 Gently fold the chopped eggs and peas into the sauce. Season to taste with salt and pepper, then return to very low heat and warm through gently. Lastly, fold in the mushrooms (see Cook's tips). Pour the mixture into the cooked pastry case. Serve hot or cold.

Cook's Notes

 TIME
Both preparation and cooking of this flan can be completed within 1 hour.

 VARIATION
Frozen cut green beans are a good alternative to frozen peas.

 SERVING IDEAS
Hot or cold, this flan is delicious with mango chutney and a crisp salad.

 COOK'S TIPS
Choose the smallest mushrooms you can find and trim the stalks level with top of caps before slicing.

Make sure the mushrooms are added to the filling at the last minute so that they do not discolour it.

● 445 calories/1865 kj per portion

Savoury bread and butter pudding

SERVES 4

6 thin slices white bread, crusts
  removed (see Economy)

40 g/1½ oz butter, softened
1 onion, finely chopped
50 g/2 oz Cheddar cheese, grated
2 eggs
1 egg yolk
300 ml/½ pint milk
salt and freshly ground black pepper
parsley sprigs, to garnish

1 Melt 15 g/½ oz of the butter in a small saucepan. Add the onion and fry gently for 5 minutes. Set aside.
2 With remaining butter grease an ovenproof dish and spread the bread. Cut each slice into 2 triangles and arrange half, butter side up, in the dish. Sprinkle over half the cheese and half the onion.
3 Arrange the remaining bread slices on top, butter side down. Sprinkle over the remaining cheese and onion. Beat eggs, egg yolk and milk together, then season to taste.
4 Slowly pour the egg mixture over the bread and butter. Cover and set aside for 30 minutes to let the bread soak (see Cook's tips).
5 Meanwhile, heat the oven to 180C/350F/Gas 4.
6 Uncover the pudding and bake just above the centre of the oven for 40-45 minutes until the top has browned and the custard has set. Garnish with parsley and serve.

Cook's Notes

TIME
Preparation 15 minutes. Soaking 30 minutes and baking 40-45 minutes.

COOK'S TIPS
Allowing the bread to absorb the liquid gives the pudding a light fluffy texture.
The pudding can be prepared up to 2 hours in advance, covered and refrigerated.

ECONOMY
Use left-over pieces of bread and butter to make this tasty supper dish.

SERVING IDEAS
Serve the savoury bread and butter pudding with a mixed salad or a seasonal green vegetable.

● 305 calories/1275 kj per portion

Cottage cheese and fruit salad

SERVES 4

1 large pear
2 bananas
juice of 1 lemon
500 g/1 lb cottage cheese
4 tablespoons thick bottled
  mayonnaise
1 small crisp lettuce (see Buying
  guide)
4 small tomatoes, quartered
½ cucumber, thinly sliced
4 carrots, grated
200 g/7 oz can sweetcorn, drained
2 peaches, sliced
25 g/1 oz raisins, to garnish

DRESSING
2 tablespoons vegetable oil
2 tablespoons red wine vinegar
good pinch of dried basil
salt and freshly ground black pepper

1 Peel, core and slice the pear, slice the bananas and then sprinkle the slices with a little lemon juice to prevent them from discolouring.

2 Mix the cottage cheese with the mayonnaise. Divide the lettuce leaves between 4 plates and pile a portion of the cottage cheese mixture in the centre of each.

3 Surround each serving of cottage cheese with the prepared vegetables and fruit, arranging the ingredients separately, in portions. Sprinkle the raisins on to the banana slices.

4 Make the dressing: put all the ingredients in a screw-top jar and shake until thoroughly blended. Sprinkle the dressing over the tomato wedges, sliced cucumber and grated carrot. Serve at once.

Cook's Notes

 TIME
Preparing the salad takes about 30 minutes.

 VARIATIONS
This salad can be made with other fruits according to seasonal availability, try sliced avocado, chunks of melon, strawberries, grapes or cherries.

● 440 calories/1850 kj per portion

 BUYING GUIDE
Crisp lettuce gives a good texture contrast to soft fruit. Choose a Webb's Wonder, cos or Iceberg.

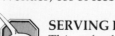 **SERVING IDEAS**
This refreshing salad is just the thing to serve for a summer lunch accompanied by a selection of crispbreads. Reduce the quantities for a quick and simple lunch for one.

Courgette and tomato mousse

SERVES 4-6

250 g/9 oz courgettes, sliced about
   1 cm/½ inch thick
25 g/1 oz margarine or butter
150 ml/¼ pint thick bottled
   mayonnaise
150 ml/¼ pint cold chicken stock
2 eggs, separated
3 tablespoons water
15 g/½ oz powdered gelatine
2 tablespoons snipped chives
few drops Tabasco (optional)
salt and freshly ground black pepper
250 g/9 oz tomatoes, skinned,
   deseeded and diced (see Cook's
   tip)

TO GARNISH
tomato slices
1 tablespoon snipped chives

1 Melt the margarine in a large frying-pan over low heat, add the courgettes and cook gently for about 15 minutes until soft, stirring so that the courgettes do not brown.
2 Place the courgettes with the mayonnaise, chicken stock and egg yolks in a blender or food processor and blend to a purée.
3 Put the water in a bowl, sprinkle over the gelatine and leave to soak until spongy. Then stand the bowl in a pan of hot water and stir until the gelatine is dissolved and the liquid is clear.
4 Turn the purée into a large bowl and stir in the chives and the Tabasco, if using. Taste and season. Then stir in the dissolved gelatine. Leave in the refrigerator for about 30 minutes until just setting.
5 Stir the purée until smooth then stir in the diced tomato. Whisk the egg whites until they stand in stiff peaks and then carefully fold into the purée.

6 Turn the mixture into a 1 L/2 pint soufflé dish and chill for about 1½ hours or until set.
7 Serve garnished with tomato slices and snipped chives.

Cook's Notes

TIME
The mousse takes about 30 minutes to prepare, allow 30 minutes for the mixture to come to setting point in the refrigerator, plus the chilling time.

COOK'S TIP
When deseeding the tomatoes, cut out the hard white piece of core under the stalk as it is rather dry and tough to eat and will spoil the texture of the mousse.

●355 calories/1500 kj per portion

Tangy egg salad

SERVES 4

4 large hard-boiled eggs
500 g/1 lb new potatoes, scrubbed or scraped
salt
250 g/9 oz shelled small fresh garden peas
3 tablespoons natural yoghurt
2 tablespoons thick bottled mayonnaise
1 tablespoon vegetable oil
75 g/3 oz Danish blue cheese, crumbled
radishes and cress sprigs, to garnish (optional)

1 Boil potatoes in salted water until tender. Drain, rinse under cold water, then drain again and halve.
2 Place the peas in a saucepan and sprinkle over ½ teaspoon salt. Pour over enough hot water to cover the peas, then simmer until nearly tender. Drain the peas, rinse under cold running water, then mix with the halved potatoes. Transfer carefully to a large serving plate.
3 Make the dressing: put the yoghurt, mayonnaise, oil and cheese in a blender or food processor and blend until smooth.
4 Cut the eggs in half and arrange them on top of the vegetables, then spoon over the dressing. Serve garnished with radishes and cress, if liked.

Cook's Notes

TIME
This salad takes 30 minutes to prepare.

SERVING IDEAS
Serve as a delicious lunch, perfect for hot summer days. This blue cheese dressing is very popular in the United States and can be used on all sorts of salads, or as a dip with crisp fresh vegetables.

●395 calories/1650 kj per portion

Snacks

Simple snacks for daytime
or evening can be combined with soup for
a quickly prepared meal that takes little time and effort
but has those touches that convenience food snacks are so lacking.
Some of the light meal suggestions here are
also suitable as starters.

Pilchard slices

SERVES 4

375 g/13 oz shortcrust pastry,
   defrosted if frozen
beaten egg, for brushing

FILLING

225 g/8 oz can pilchards in tomato
   sauce, drained and tomato sauce
   reserved (see Serving ideas)
1 cooking apple
1 onion, coarsely grated
1 teaspoon dried mixed herbs
salt and freshly ground black pepper

1 Heat the oven to 200C/400F/Gas 6.
2 Prepare the filling: lay the
pilchards on a plate and split each in
half lengthways. Carefully remove
the backbones then mash pilchards
with fork. Transfer to a clean bowl.
3 Peel and coarsely grate the apple
and mix with the onion and herbs.
Season with salt and pepper. Add to
the pilchards and mix well.
4 On a lightly floured board,
roll out the pastry to a rectangle 32½ × 24½ cm/13 × 10
inches, reserving the trimmings.
Cut the rectangle into 2 to make
a rectangle of 32½ × 11 cm/13 ×
4½ inches and another of 32½ ×
13½ cm/13 × 5½ inches.
5 Put the smaller rectangle on a
baking sheet. Spread the pilchard
mixture in 4 strips across the pastry
(see Preparation). Brush the edges
with egg and place the larger pastry
rectangle on top. Press down
between fish strips. Crimp edges to
prevent juices escaping. Roll out
trimmings and cut out 4 fish (see
Preparation).
6 Brush the slice with egg and place
the fish on top. Bake above the
centre of the oven for 25-30 minutes
until well browned. Slice the pastry
between each strip of fish mixture.
Serve hot or cold.

Cook's Notes

TIME
Preparation takes about
30 minutes. Cooking
time is 30 minutes.

SERVING IDEAS
Serve hot with peas and
carrots and a sauce
made using the tomato sauce
from the pilchard can, 15 g/½ oz
margarine, 15 g/½ oz plain
flour, 150 ml/¼ pint milk, 1
tablespoon tomato ketchup and
¼ teaspoon Worcestershire
sauce.

PREPARATION
To prepare the pastry
slices:

1 Using a knife, spread the pilchard
mixture in 4 even strips across the
smaller rectangle of pastry.

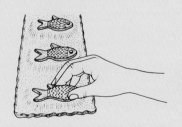

2 Cut out 4 fish and 4 circles for
eyes. Mark scales with the point of
a knife if wished. Brush the slice
with egg and arrange a fish on
each portion of pilchard mixture.

●540 calories/2275 kj per portion

Scrambled smoky

SERVES 4

500 g/1 lb smoked haddock fillets, defrosted if frozen
150 ml/¼ pint milk
8 large eggs
salt
cayenne pepper
50 g/2 oz butter
1 teaspoon Worcestershire sauce
8 large slices French bread
butter, for spreading
parsley, to garnish

1 Put the fish in a large saucepan. Reserve 2 tablespoons milk, mix the rest with a little water and pour enough of the mixture over the fish just to cover it. Cook gently for 15-20 minutes. If using frozen fish, cook according to packet instructions.
2 Drain the fish and flake it into a bowl, discarding any bones or skin. Set aside while you cook the eggs.

3 Beat the eggs in a bowl with the reserved milk and season with a little salt and cayenne pepper to taste.
4 Melt the butter in a saucepan or large frying-pan, add the beaten eggs and cook over gentle heat, stirring all the time, until the eggs are just scrambled but still creamy.
! Stir in the flaked fish and the Worcestershire sauce. Taste and adjust seasoning.
5 Toast the bread, butter one side, then pile the egg and fish mixture on to the toast. Garnish with parsley and serve at once.

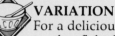

Cook's Notes

TIME
This tasty variation of scrambled eggs takes about 30 minutes to prepare and cook.

WATCHPOINT
The eggs will continue to cook from the heat in the saucepan after they are removed from the cooker. Take them off just before they are ready.

SERVING IDEAS
The egg and fish mixture can be piled into a warmed serving dish, slices of toast cut into triangles and arranged around the edge of the dish.
This makes a substantial breakfast dish, perfect for a Sunday morning.
Serve with a tomato salad for lunch or supper.

VARIATION
For a delicious addition to the flaked fish, try 50 g/2 oz sliced mushrooms softened in a little butter.

●700 calories/2925 kj per portion

Kipper and tomato rolls

MAKES 6

200 g/7 oz frozen kipper fillets
25 g/1 oz margarine or butter
1 large onion, sliced
200 g/7 oz can tomatoes
1 bay leaf
salt and freshly ground black pepper
1 tablespoon cornflour
150 ml/¼ pint water
1 tablespoon chopped fresh parsley
6 large round crusty rolls

1 Heat the oven to 200C/400F/Gas 6 and cut out 6 pieces of foil large enough to parcel the rolls.
2 Cook the kippers according to packet instructions.
3 Meanwhile, melt the margarine in a frying-pan. Add the onion and fry gently for 5 minutes until soft and lightly coloured.
4 Remove from the heat and stir in the tomatoes, including their juice. Add the bay leaf and seasoning.
5 In a bowl, blend the cornflour with a little of the water until smooth. Stir in the remainder, then add to the pan.
6 Return to the heat and bring to the boil, stirring constantly and breaking up the tomatoes with a spoon. Simmer uncovered over low to moderate heat for 10 minutes, stirring frequently until the sauce is thick. Remove the bay leaf and stir in the parsley.
7 Drain the fish and, when cool enough to handle, skin, bone and flake the flesh. Add the fish to the sauce, taste and adjust seasoning.
8 Cut off the tops of the rolls and scoop out the centres (see Economy).
9 Spoon the sauce into the rolls, replace the lids, wrap each one in foil and place on a baking sheet. Bake in the oven for 8-10 minutes, leave to cool for a few minutes, then unwrap and serve hot.

Cook's Notes

 TIME
Preparation takes 20 minutes. Cooking time is about 30 minutes.

 SERVING IDÉAS
Serve with a salad of lettuce, sliced cucumber and green pepper.

 VARIATIONS
Use a French loaf instead of rolls: cut the top off the loaf, scoop out the centre and fill. Vol-au-vent cases can also be filled with this mixture. For a different flavour, replace some of the parsley with other chopped fresh herbs such as thyme or basil.

 ECONOMY
Make breadcrumbs from the roll centres that are not needed; they can be stored in the freezer in a polythene bag for up to 3 months.

●210 calories/880 kj per roll

Frankfurter puffs

MAKES 8
250 g/9 oz frankfurters, sliced
**50 g/2 oz frozen mixed vegetables
  (see Economy)**
salt and freshly ground black pepper
215 g/7½ oz can baked beans
**400 g/13 oz frozen puff pastry,
  defrosted**
2 tablespoons water
vegetable oil, for deep frying
watercress, to garnish

1 Bring a small pan of salted water to the boil and cook the mixed vegetables for 3 minutes. Drain.
2 Mix together the frankfurters, beans and mixed vegetables, season to taste with salt and pepper.
3 On a lightly floured surface, roll out the pastry to a 48 × 24 cm/ 20 × 10 inch rectangle. Cut in half lengthways and then divide each of

the halves into four equal-sized 12 cm/5 inch squares.
4 Heat the oven to 110C/225F/Gas ¼.
5 Put a spoonful of sausage mixture on to each piece of pastry, dampen the edges and fold each corner over into the middle to form parcels. Pinch along the edges to seal.
6 Pour enough oil into a deep-fat frier to cover the sausage parcels.

Heat to 180C/350F or until a stale bread cube browns in 60 seconds.
7 Using a slotted spoon, lower 4 parcels into hot oil and deep fry for 10 minutes until evenly golden brown all over. Drain on absorbent paper and keep warm while frying the remainder (see Cook's tip). Serve them at once, garnished with watercress sprigs.

120

Curried chicken toasts

SERVES 4

2 cooked chicken pieces, each weighing about 250 g/9 oz

225 g/8 oz can pineapple cubes, drained

3 tablespoons thick bottled mayonnaise

3 tablespoons soured cream

50 g/2 oz black grapes, halved and deseeded

1 tablespoon lemon juice

2 teaspoons curry paste (see Cook's tip)

salt and freshly ground black pepper

4 slices crusty bread

25 g/1 oz margarine or butter

thin tomato and cucumber slices, to garnish

1 Remove the skin and bones from the chicken and chop the flesh.

2 Heat the grill to high.

3 Put the chicken, pineapple, mayonnaise, soured cream, grapes, lemon juice and curry paste into a saucepan and stir well to mix. Season to taste with salt and pepper.

4 Stir over low heat for 5 minutes until the mixture is heated through.

5 Meanwhile, toast the bread until golden on both sides and spread one side of each slice with margarine.

6 Spoon the chicken mixture on to the toast, dividing it equally between the 4 slices. Serve at once, garnished with tomato and cucumber slices.

Cook's Notes

 TIME
15 minutes to prepare, 10 minutes cooking.

 VARIATIONS
Substitute the mayonnaise with 2 tablespoons single cream to make a creamy sauce. For a hot buffet snack, toast slices of French bread and spread with chicken mixture.

 COOK'S TIP
Curry paste should be used rather than curry powder in this recipe, because it does not need such a long cooking time. If curry powder is not cooked long enough, the finished dish tends to taste gritty and raw.

●360 calories/1500 kj per portion

Salmon mousse

SERVES 4-6

200 g/7 oz can pink or red salmon, drained, with juice reserved
225-250 ml/8-9 fl oz milk
25 g/1 oz margarine or butter
25 g/1 oz plain flour
2 eggs, separated
1 rounded tablespoon (1 sachet) powdered gelatine
2 tablespoons lemon juice
2 tablespoons water
2 tablespoons tomato ketchup
150 ml/¼ pint single cream
salt and freshly ground black pepper
sprigs of dill
cucumber slices, to garnish

1 Strain the juice from the salmon into a measuring jug and make up to 300 ml/½ pint with milk.
2 Melt the margarine in a small saucepan, sprinkle in the flour and stir over low heat for 1-2 minutes

until straw-coloured. Remove from the heat and gradually stir in the milk mixture. Return to the heat and simmer, stirring, until thick and smooth.
3 Remove from the heat and stir in the egg yolks.
4 Mash the fish roughly with a fork, discarding all skin and bones. Stir into the sauce, then work the mixture in a blender for a few seconds until smooth. Pour into a clean bowl and set aside to cool.
5 Sprinkle the gelatine over the lemon juice and water in a small heatproof bowl. Leave to soak for 5 minutes until spongy then stand the bowl in a pan of gently simmering water for 1-2 minutes, stirring occasionally, until the gelatine has dissolved.
6 Remove from the heat, leave to cool slightly, then stir into the salmon mixture with the tomato ketchup and cream. Season to taste with salt and pepper. Cover and refrigerate for 2-3 hours, or until on the point of setting.
7 In a clean, dry bowl, whisk the

egg whites until standing in stiff peaks, then fold into salmon mixture with a large metal spoon.
8 Line base of an oiled 850 ml/1½ pint ring mould with dill sprigs. Spoon salmon mixture carefully on top. Refrigerate overnight.
9 Dip base of mould in hot water for 10 seconds, then turn mousse out on to a serving plate. Serve chilled, garnished with cucumber.

Savoury aubergine slices

SERVES 4

2 large aubergines
salt
1 egg
6 tablespoons fresh breadcrumbs
8 tablespoons vegetable or
    sunflower oil
2 cloves garlic, crushed (optional)
250 g/9 oz smoked streaky bacon
    rashers, rinds removed and
    chopped
2 bunches spring onions, chopped
4 slices white bread, crusts removed
    and cut into 1 cm/½ inch dice
2 tablespoons chopped fresh
    parsley
freshly ground black pepper

1 Cut the aubergines into 1 cm/½ inch slices and put them in a colander in layers, sprinkling salt between each layer. Cover with a plate and place a heavy weight on top. Leave for about 1 hour to draw out the bitter juices, then rinse the slices under cold running water and pat dry on absorbent paper.

2 Heat the oven to 110C/225F/Gas ¼.

3 Beat the egg in a shallow dish and spread the breadcrumbs out on a large flat plate. Dip each aubergine slice into the beaten egg and then into the breadcrumbs until evenly coated.

4 Heat 3 tablespoons oil in a large frying-pan (see Cook's tip), add half the aubergine slices and fry for 3-4 minutes on each side until they are golden brown. Remove from the pan and drain on absorbent paper. Keep warm in the oven while you fry the remainder in 3 more tablespoons oil.

5 When all the aubergines are cooked, heat the remaining 2 tablespoons oil in the same pan, add the crushed garlic, if using, the bacon, spring onions and diced bread. Fry for 8-10 minutes, stirring occasionally until the bacon is crisp and the bread golden brown. Stir in the parsley and season with salt and pepper. [!]

6 Arrange the aubergine slices on a warmed serving dish and sprinkle with the bacon, onion and bread mixture. Serve at once.

Deep-fried ravioli

MAKES 30
225 g/8 oz plain flour
large pinch salt
50 g/2 oz butter, diced
2 eggs, separated
75 ml/3 fl oz water
vegetable oil, for deep frying
basil leaves, to garnish

FILLING
75 g/3 oz Gruyère cheese, finely
   diced
75 g/3 oz cooked ham, finely
   chopped
1 tablespoon finely chopped fresh
   parsley
1 tablespoon chopped fresh basil
1 egg
salt and freshly ground black pepper

1 Make the filling: mix together the cheese, ham and herbs in a medium-sized bowl. In another bowl beat the egg with a little salt and freshly ground black pepper. Cover both and refrigerate.

2 Sift the flour and salt into a large bowl. Add the butter and rub it in with the fingertips until the mixture resembles fine breadcrumbs. Make a well in the centre, add egg yolks and water and mix to a soft dough.
3 Turn out on to a lightly floured surface and knead gently until dough is no longer sticky. Roll out to a rectangle about 38 × 25 cm/ 15 × 10 inches and cut out about thirty 6.5 cm/2½ inch circles.
4 Lightly beat the egg whites. Brush the edges of the circles with the egg whites and place a teaspoon of the filling in the centre of each one. Fold each over the edges, to form semi-circles. Press the edges together to seal.
5 Meanwhile, pour enough oil into a deep-fat frier with a basket to come halfway up the sides. Heat the oil to 190C/375F or until a stale bread cube turns golden in 50 seconds. Fry ravioli, in batches of 10, until golden brown.
6 Remove and drain on absorbent paper. Fry the remaining ravioli, reheating the oil between batches. Pile the cooked ravioli on to a serving plate and serve at once, garnished with basil leaves.

Cook's Notes

 TIME
Making the dough and filling take 15 minutes. Filling the ravioli with its cheese and ham stuffing takes about 10 minutes and deep-frying 10-15 minutes.

 SERVING IDEAS
Serve with a salad of thinly sliced Mozzarella cheese and tomato, sprinkled with a little olive oil, seasoning and extra chopped herbs.

VARIATION
If fresh basil is not available use an extra tablespoon of chopped parsley.

? DID YOU KNOW
This recipe is a variation of the Italian *panzarotti alla Romana*. The dough is a type of simple pasta. The Italians often use pasta in this way as a sort of batter.

 ●70 calories/300 kj per ravioli

Creamy roes

SERVES 4

350 g/12 oz soft herring roes
40 g/1½ oz plain flour
salt and freshly ground black pepper
25 g/1 oz margarine or butter
8 slices wholemeal bread
4 tablespoons double cream
1 tablespoon lemon juice
2 tablespoons snipped chives (see Buying guide)
1 tablespoon chopped fresh parsley
orange and lemon slices, to garnish

1 Wash the roes well, drain and pat dry on absorbent paper.
2 Put the flour in a polythene bag and season with salt and pepper. Add the roes and shake until they are evenly coated.
3 Heat the grill to high.
4 Melt the margarine in a frying-pan, add the roes and cook over moderate heat for 7-10 minutes or until the roes are cooked and a golden brown colour.
5 Meanwhile, cut each bread slice into a large round using a pastry cutter or saucer as a guide. Toast on both sides and keep warm.
6 Stir the cream, lemon juice, chives and parsley into the roes and season with salt and pepper. Cook over low heat for 1 minute.
7 Place 2 bread rounds on each of 4 warmed serving plates so that they overlap. Spoon over the creamy roes. Garnish with orange and lemon slices and serve at once.

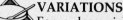

Cook's Notes

 TIME
10 minutes to prepare and about 10 minutes cooking time.

 BUYING GUIDE
If fresh chives are unavailable, use chopped spring onion leaves instead.

 SERVING IDEAS
Serve on sliced rye bread and garnish with lettuce leaves as a tasty starter to a dinner party followed by a light main course.

VARIATIONS
For a less rich sauce, use single cream. Soured cream can be used, but omit the lemon juice. To make the dish more peppery, sprinkle with a little cayenne before serving. Other fresh chopped herbs can be used such as thyme, sage or tarragon, but use the herbs sparingly as the delicate flavour of the herring roes can be easily masked by adding too much.

●345 calories/1450 kj per portion

Ham and pineapple croissants

SERVES 4

4 slices ham, total weight about 100 g/4 oz
4 canned pineapple rings, drained
4 croissants
50 g/2 oz butter, softened
½ teaspoon made English mustard
2 tablespoons mango chutney, chopped

1 Heat the oven to 190C/375F/Gas 5. Cut 4 pieces of foil large enough to enclose a croissant completely.
2 Split the croissants through the rounded side, without cutting through the pointed ends.
3 Mix the butter with the mustard and spread it inside the croissants. Cut the pineapple rings in half, and arrange 2 halves on the bottom half of each croissant (see Cook's tips and Preparation).
4 Spread the ham slices with chutney, roll them up diagonally and put on top of the pineapple. Press down the croissant tops, then wrap each croissant in foil.
5 Put the foil parcels on a baking sheet and heat in the oven for about 15 minutes. Serve hot or just warm.

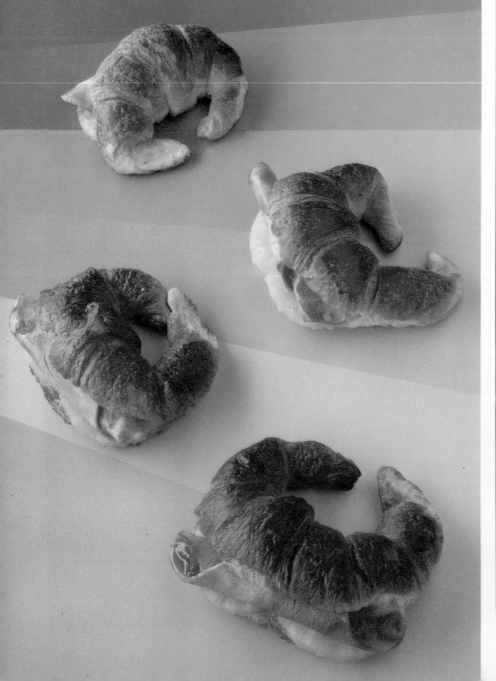

Cook's Notes

TIME
Preparation and warming through take about 25 minutes.

VARIATIONS
Sliced tongue, salt beef or chopped ham with pork can be used instead of ham. Use other drained canned fruit such as apricots, apple slices or peaches. Vary the chutney, but choose only the milder ones, or the buttery flavour of the croissant will be overpowered.

COOK'S TIPS
Croissants vary in size and shape so the pineapple rings and ham have to be cut to the most suitable shape to tuck into the croissant without looking unsightly.
The filled croissants can be prepared and refrigerated in advance, but the fruit must be well drained or the croissants will become soggy.

SERVING IDEAS
Serve the hot croissants in napkins as a snack—they are ideal for parties—or on a plate with a tossed mixed salad for a main meal.

PREPARATION
To split and fill the croissants:

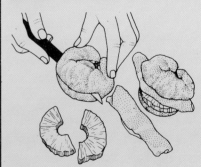

1 *Split the croissants through their rounded side without cutting right through their pointed ends. Arrange 2 halves of pineapple ring on the bottom half of each croissant and top with a ham roll.*

●455 calories/1900 kj per portion

Ribbon loaf

SERVES 6-8

350 g/12 oz full-fat soft cheese
1½ tablespoons chopped fresh
    parsley
2 teaspoons snipped chives
1 clove garlic, crushed (optional)
salt and freshly ground black pepper
few drops of green and red food
    colouring
115 g/4¼ oz can sardines, drained
1 tablespoon lemon juice
2 eggs, hard-boiled and shelled
2 tablespoons thick bottled
    mayonnaise
75 g/3 oz Cheddar cheese, finely
    grated
1 teaspoon tomato purée
1-2 tablespoons milk
1 day-old small white tin loaf
softened butter, for spreading
4 radishes, to garnish

1 Place a quarter of the soft cheese in a small bowl. Stir in the parsley, chives and garlic, if using, and season to taste with salt and pepper. Mix together well, then add the green food colouring a drop at a time, mixing it in until the cheese is coloured a light green. Set aside.
2 Put the remaining soft cheese in a separate bowl and beat with a wooden spoon until smooth. Add the red food colouring until the cheese is coloured pink. Set aside.
3 Mash the sardines with the lemon juice in a separate bowl. Taste and season with salt and pepper. Mix until smooth and set aside.
4 In another bowl, mash the eggs with the mayonnaise until smooth. Season to taste and set aside.
5 Mash the grated Cheddar with the tomato purée and milk to make a spreading consistency. Set aside.
6 Carefully cut off and discard the rounded top of the loaf and then remove the crusts. Cut the loaf horizontally into 5 equal slices.
7 Spread 1 slice of bread with butter, then with the green herb cheese mixture. Butter another slice of bread and spread the sardine mixture on it. Place on top of the first slice. Repeat with a third slice, using the egg mixture, then with a fourth slice, using the Cheddar cheese mixture.
8 Butter the remaining slice of bread, then place buttered-side down on top. Press down gently.
9 Carefully cover the loaf all over with the pink cream cheese mixture.
10 Cover with cling film and refrigerate for several hours.
11 Remove from the refrigerator 30 minutes before eating. Garnish with radish accordions (see Preparation). Serve sliced. ⚠

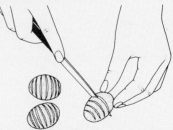

Fun fish cakes

SERVES 4

350 g/12 oz smoked cod fillet, skinned
350 g/12 oz potatoes, boiled and mashed
2 tablespoons snipped chives
1 egg yolk
salt and freshly ground black pepper
3 tablespoons plain flour
1 egg, beaten
75 g/3 oz golden breadcrumbs
25 g/1 oz margarine or butter, melted
2 stuffed olives, halved
vegetable oil, for greasing
parsley and lemon wedges, to garnish

1 Heat the oven to 200C/400F/Gas 6. Generously grease a large baking sheet.

2 Put the fish in a large saucepan and cover with cold water. Bring to the boil, then lower the heat and simmer very gently for about 10 minutes.

3 Remove the fish from the pan with a slotted spoon and cool.

4 Flake the flesh of the cooked fish, discarding any bones, and mix it very thoroughly with the potato, chives and egg yolk. Season with salt and pepper.

5 Divide the mixture into 4 equal portions and with floured hands shape into flat pear shapes about 2.5 cm/1 inch thick. Shape the thinner end of the cakes to form a 'V', like the tail of a fish.

6 Put the egg in a shallow bowl and spread the breadcrumbs out on a flat plate. Dip the cakes in the beaten egg then in the breadcrumbs until thoroughly and evenly coated.

7 Place the fish cakes on the prepared baking sheet, then drizzle the melted margarine evenly over them. Bake in the oven for 20-25 minutes until crisp and golden brown.

8 To serve: transfer the fish cakes to a serving platter, then place the stuffed olive halves on one side of the fish to represent eyes and decorate with parsley and lemon wedges.

Cook's Notes

TIME
Preparation time, including cooking the fish, takes 25 minutes. Baking takes about 25 minutes.

VARIATION
Add a little lemon zest and a few chopped prawns to the mashed potato and fish mixture. Add 2 tablespoons grated Parmesan cheese to the breadcrumbs.

FREEZING
Cool the baked fish cakes quickly. Open freeze them on a tray, then pack in polythene bags and seal, label and freeze. Store for up to 1 month. To serve: defrost at room temperature for about 4 hours, then reheat in a 200C/400F/Gas 6 oven for about 10 minutes until hot.

●320 calories/1350 kj per portion

Tea-time scramble

SERVES 4

 250 g/9 oz chipolata sausages
8 large day-old slices white bread
 3-4 tablespoons vegetable oil
6 eggs
3 tablespoons milk
salt and freshly ground black pepper
25 g/1 oz margarine or butter

1 Heat the oven to 110C/225F/Gas ¼. Heat the grill to moderate and grill the sausages for 10-15 minutes, turning as necessary, until well browned and cooked through.
2 Meanwhile, using fancy biscuit cutters (see Cook's tip and Economy), cut out 8 shapes from 4 of the bread slices.
3 Heat the vegetable oil in a large frying-pan, add the bread shapes and the remaining 4 bread slices and fry, turning as necessary, until golden brown and crisp on both sides. Drain on absorbent paper and keep hot in the oven.
4 Cut the sausages into thin slices and set aside until required.
5 Beat the eggs in a bowl with the milk and season to taste.
6 Melt the margarine in a heavy-based saucepan. Add the beaten egg mixture and sliced sausages and cook gently, stirring until the eggs are lightly scrambled and still soft and creamy.
7 Put the slices of fried bread on individual plates and pile the egg and sausage mixture on to them, dividing it equally between them. Place 2 fried bread shapes on top of each slice and serve at once.

Cook's Notes

 TIME
This children's special takes only about 25 minutes to prepare and cook.

ECONOMY
The remaining bread crusts left after cutting out the shapes may be made into breadcrumbs and stored in an airtight container in the freezer for up to 3 months.

 **VARIATION**
The egg and sausage mixture may be served on buttered toast and topped with a toasted shape.

COOK'S TIP
Use a really sharp cutter with a bold outline and avoid making very small shapes as they will shrink slightly during cooking.

 SERVING IDEAS
This tasty dish makes a nutritious tea-time treat for children. Serve the eggs and sausages with baked beans, grilled tomatoes and glasses of chilled apple juice. Round off the meal with a selection of fresh fruit, fruit-flavoured yoghurt or canned fruit.

●435 calories/1825 kj per portion

Savoury sausage cake

MAKES 8 WEDGES

500 g/1 lb pork sausagemeat
50 g/2 oz plain flour
4 tablespoons milk
1 egg, lightly beaten
1 medium onion, finely chopped
1 large apple, peeled and roughly
** diced**
1 tablespoon tomato purée
½ teaspoon dried sage
salt and freshly ground black pepper
margarine, for greasing
tomato slices, to garnish

1 Heat the oven to 190C/375F/Gas 5 and then generously grease a large sandwich tin with margarine.
2 Sift the flour into a large bowl.

Add the remaining ingredients, including the sausagemeat, and season generously with salt and freshly ground black pepper. Knead together well with the hands, until well mixed and of an even consistency throughout.

3 Press mixture flat in the sandwich tin, and bake in the oven for 40 minutes until the top is golden brown. Leave cake to cool slightly, then turn on to a warmed serving plate and garnish with tomato. Serve sliced (see Serving ideas).

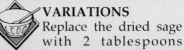

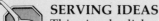

TIME
Preparation takes about 10 minutes and cooking time is about 40 minutes.

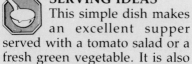

VARIATIONS
Replace the dried sage with 2 tablespoons chopped fresh parsley.
Chop 2 celery stalks into the mixture and/or add 50 g/2 oz chopped cooked rashers of bacon with the rind removed.

SERVING IDEAS
This simple dish makes an excellent supper served with a tomato salad or a fresh green vegetable. It is also an interesting accompaniment to left-over poultry and game.
Alternatively, left to cool completely, this sausage cake makes a very tasty and filling picnic or packed lunch snack.

●230 calories/950 kj per portion

130

Bacon and mushroom scone roll

SERVES 8

100 g/4 oz bacon rashers, chopped
100 g/4 oz mushrooms, chopped
75 g/3 oz margarine
1 small onion, finely chopped
225 g/8 oz self-raising flour
¼ teaspoon mustard powder
pinch of salt
50 g/2 oz Cheddar cheese, grated
150 ml/¼ pint milk
beaten egg, to glaze
vegetable oil, for greasing

1 Heat the oven to 220C/425F/Gas 7. Grease a baking sheet.
2 Melt 25 g/1 oz of the margarine in a frying-pan, add the onion and fry gently for about 5 minutes until soft and lightly coloured. Add the bacon and fry for a further 1 minute, then add the mushrooms and cook until all the moisture has evaporated (5-10 minutes). Remove from the heat and leave the mixture to cool.
3 Meanwhile, make the scone dough: sift the flour, mustard and salt into a bowl. Rub in the remaining margarine, add the cheese, and gradually mix in the milk until a soft dough is formed.
4 Turn the dough on to a floured surface, knead lightly, then roll out to a 20 cm/8 inch square. Spread the mushroom mixture over the scone dough, leaving a 2 cm/¾ inch margin along the edge furthest away from you. Brush the margin with a little of the beaten egg. Starting with the edge nearest you firmly roll up the dough like a Swiss roll and press the edge firmly to seal.
5 Place the roll on the prepared baking sheet with the seam underneath. Brush with the remaining beaten egg and bake in the oven for 30 minutes or until golden brown. Trim ends, if wished, and cut into slices to serve (see Serving ideas).

Cook's Notes

TIME
Preparation and baking take about 50 minutes.

SERVING IDEAS
This scone roll makes a very substantial snack served hot with grilled tomatoes or baked beans. Served cold, it makes good picnic fare.

VARIATION
Chopped green peppers may be added to the filling instead of bacon.

● 250 calories/1050 kj per portion

Crab toasties

SERVES 4

175 g/6 oz can crabmeat, drained and flaked (see Buying guide)
75 ml/3 fl oz soured cream
1 tablespoon French mustard
1 tablespoon Worcestershire sauce
1 tablespoon lemon juice
salt and freshly ground black pepper
4 slices brown bread
butter, for spreading
25 g/1 oz Cheddar cheese, grated
tomato slices, to garnish
parsley sprigs, to garnish

1 Heat the grill to high.
2 Mix the crabmeat, soured cream, mustard, Worcestershire sauce and lemon juice together in a saucepan and season to taste with salt and pepper. Heat gently for about 5 minutes without boiling, stirring the mixture occasionally.
3 Meanwhile, toast the brown bread and then spread each slice evenly with the butter.
4 Spread the crab mixture over the toast, sprinkle over the grated cheese and brown under the grill. Serve at once, garnished with tomato slices and parsley sprigs.

Cook's Notes

TIME
Preparation and cooking take 10 minutes.

SERVING IDEAS
The same mixture can be used to fill individual pre-baked pastry or vol-au-vent cases without the cheese topping. Or serve as a starter in individual soufflé or ramekin dishes. Or brown the mixture under the grill and serve with fingers of hot toast.

BUYING GUIDE
You can use the same weight of frozen crabmeat, but defrost it completely before using.

●250 calories/1050 kj per portion

Summer salmon pies

SERVES 4
105 g/3¾ oz can red salmon,
    drained and flaked
215 g/7½ oz frozen shortcrust
    pastry, defrosted
1 small onion, very finely chopped
2 teaspoons snipped chives
150 g/5 oz natural yoghurt
2 eggs
150 ml/¼ pint milk
salt and freshly ground black pepper

1 Heat the oven to 200C/400F/Gas 6.
2 Roll out the pastry thinly on a lightly floured surface. Cut out four 12 cm/5 inch circles, using a saucer or small plate as a guide.
3 Press each circle into a 10 cm/4 inch small deep tart tin (see Cook's tip). Ease the pastry into the base and press into the sides. Trim off any excess pastry and prick the bases with a fork. Cover and refrigerate for 15 minutes.

4 Meanwhile, make the filling: mix the salmon, onion and chives together in a bowl. In a jug, beat the yoghurt and eggs together until smooth, then gradually stir in the milk. Season with salt and pepper.
5 Divide salmon mixture equally between pastry cases, spreading it evenly over the base. Pour the yoghurt mixture over the salmon, filling each case almost to the top.
6 Place the tart tins on a baking sheet and bake in the oven for 40-45 minutes until golden.
7 Transfer to a serving plate and serve warm or cold.

Cook's Notes

 TIME
Preparation takes 30-40 minutes; baking takes 40-45 minutes.

FREEZING
Cool the pies completely, then open freeze in the tins until solid. Remove from the tins, then wrap individually in foil and pack together in a rigid container. Seal, label and return to the freezer for up to 3 months. To serve: defrost in foil wrapping at room temperature for 3 hours.

●300 calories/1250 kj per portion

SERVING IDEAS
If serving cold, leave the pies to cool in the tins for 5 minutes, then transfer to a wire rack and leave until cold. Pack and take on a picnic and serve with a salad made of lettuce, tomatoes, green peppers and spring onions.

COOK'S TIP
For best results, use individual tart tins about 10 cm/4 inches wide and just under 2.5 cm/1 inch deep. These have straighter sides than trays of tarts. They also hold more filling.

Liver-stuffed tomatoes

SERVES 4

100 g/4 oz chicken livers, finely
  chopped
8 firm tomatoes
1 tablespoon vegetable oil
1 onion, finely chopped
2 bacon rashers, rinds removed and
  finely chopped
100 g/4 oz mushrooms, finely
  chopped
salt and freshly ground black pepper
75 g/3 oz fresh soft white
  breadcrumbs
1 teaspoon dried thyme
1 tablespoon finely chopped fresh
  parsley
25 g/1 oz margarine or butter
vegetable oil, for greasing
parsley sprigs, to garnish

1 Heat the oven to 180C/350F/Gas 4
and lightly oil a baking sheet.
2 Cut the tops off the tomatoes and
set aside. Use a small serrated knife
to loosen the tomato flesh, then
carefully scoop out the insides of the
tomatoes (see Economy), making
sure that you do not pierce the
skins.
3 Heat the oil in a frying-pan. Add
the onion and fry for 3-4 minutes
until soft but not coloured. Add the
bacon and mushrooms and cook for
a further 2-3 minutes. Finally add
the chicken livers and cook for about
5 minutes until well browned,
stirring all the time. Season with salt
and pepper to taste and stir in the
breadcrumbs, thyme and parsley.
4 Divide the filling between the
tomatoes. Replace the lids, arrange
on the baking sheet and dot each
with margarine. Bake in the oven for
15 minutes.
5 Using a large spoon, transfer the
tomatoes to a warmed serving dish
and serve hot, garnished with
parsley sprigs.

Chinese omelette

SERVES 4
250 g/9 oz lean pork fillet
 (tenderloin), cut into thin strips
vegetable oil, for frying
½ small green pepper, deseeded
 and finely shredded
100 g/4 oz fresh beansprouts
1 tablespoon soy sauce
salt and freshly ground black pepper
8 eggs
3 tablespoons water

1 Heat oven to 110C/225F/Gas ¼.
2 Heat 1 tablespoon oil in a large frying-pan, add the pork and fry for 2-3 minutes, stirring all the time, until the meat has lost all its pinkness.
3 Add the green pepper and cook for a further minute, then add the beansprouts and soy sauce. Cook

for a further minute, stirring all the time. Remove from the heat, taste and add salt and pepper, if necessary, and keep warm in the oven while preparing and cooking the omelette.
4 Beat the eggs with the water in a bowl and season with plenty of salt and pepper. Heat a very little oil in a large non-stick frying-pan (see Cook's tips) and when it is just beginning to sizzle, pour in the egg mixture.
5 Cook the omelette over high heat, drawing the edges towards the centre with a spatula as the omelette begins to set, and letting the uncooked egg run underneath. When the omelette is cooked (see Cook's tips), spread the pork mixture over one-half of the omelette and fold the other half over, with a fish slice, to enclose the filling.
6 Slide the omelette out of the pan on to a plate, cut into 4 portions and serve at once.

French toast sandwiches

MAKES 8

8 large slices stale bread
100-175 g/4-6 oz butter
2 teaspoons made English mustard (optional)
100-175 g/4-6 oz cooked chicken, thinly sliced
4 slices processed cheese
2 eggs
175 ml/6 fl oz milk
salt and freshly ground black pepper (see Variations)
2-3 teaspoons vegetable oil
gherkin and tomato slices, to garnish

1 Heat oven to 110C/225F/Gas ¼.
2 Spread the bread on 1 side with about half of the butter, and mustard, if liked. Place a slice of chicken and a slice of cheese on 4 of the slices of bread. Cover with the remaining bread, buttered side down, and press firmly to seal in the filling. Cut each sandwich in half diagonally.
3 Whisk the eggs lightly with the milk and salt and pepper in a shallow dish.
4 Heat 50 g/2 oz of the remaining butter and 2 teaspoons oil in a large heavy-based frying-pan until sizzling. !
5 Dip half the sandwiches in the egg and milk mixture, turning them over several times so that the bread is well coated. Fry over high heat until brown on one side, then lower the heat slightly, turn the sandwiches over and brown on the other side. Drain on absorbent paper and keep hot on a serving dish in the oven.
6 Dip and fry the remaining sandwiches in the same way, adding more butter and oil if necessary. Serve at once, garnished with gherkin and tomato slices.

Cook's Notes

TIME
Preparation and cooking take 15 minutes.

WATCHPOINT
The fat must be very hot, but not brown, when the sandwiches are added.

VARIATIONS
For a different flavour, add celery or garlic salt, sweet paprika, dried mixed herbs or a pinch of mild curry powder to the egg and milk mixture, and vary the filling as you wish. Alternatively, make sweet sandwiches: add ½ teaspoon each of caster sugar and vanilla flavouring to the egg mixture in place of salt and pepper and use a sweet filling.

●345 calories/1460 kj per portion

Chilli sausage burgers

SERVES 4-6
500 g/1 lb pork sausagemeat
1 medium onion, grated
1 large carrot, grated
50 g/2 oz fresh white breadcrumbs
4 tablespoons tomato ketchup
1 tablespoon chilli seasoning (see
　Did you know)
¼ teaspoon ground mixed spice
salt and freshly ground black pepper
vegetable oil, for frying

1 Combine all the ingredients (except the oil) in a large bowl, using floured fingertips to mix well. Season with salt and pepper.
2 With floured hands, ! divide the mixture into 4-6 portions and roll them into balls. Flatten each

slightly. Chill the burgers in the refrigerator for 30 minutes, then leave at room temperature for a few minutes before cooking (see Cook's tip).
3 Heat a little oil in a large frying-pan. Fry the burgers for 3-4 minutes on each side or until they are browned and cooked through.
4 Drain the cooked burgers thoroughly on absorbent paper, then serve at once while very hot.

Cook's Notes

TIME
Preparation 15 minutes, cooking 6-8 minutes.

COOK'S TIP
Chilling the burgers before cooking improves both their flavour and texture.

WATCHPOINT
The sausagemeat mixture is very sticky, so flour your hands well before shaping the burgers.

SERVING IDEAS
Serve the burgers with French fries and a salad, or in soft baps like hamburgers.

DID YOU KNOW
Chilli seasoning is one of the hottest flavourings for food (although not as hot as real chilli powder). It is a mixture of garlic, dried powdered chilli pepper and herbs and spices such as oregano and cumin.

●570 calories/2400 kj per portion

Pork pasties

 MAKES 4
400 g/13 oz shortcrust pastry,
 defrosted if frozen
 175 g/6 oz minced pork
1 onion, finely chopped
1 dessert apple, peeled, cored and
 chopped
½ teaspoon dried thyme
salt and freshly ground black pepper
beaten egg, to glaze
vegetable oil, for greasing

1 Heat the oven to 200C/400F/Gas 6.
2 In a bowl mix together the pork, onion, apple, thyme and salt and pepper to taste. Stir well to combine all the ingredients.
3 Roll out the pastry on a lightly floured surface into a large round, then using a 15 cm/6 inch plate or saucer as a guide, cut out 4 pastry circles.
4 Divide the filling between the rounds, placing it in the centre of each. Brush the edges of pastry with beaten egg and press them together over the top of the filling to seal. Flute the edges (see Preparation) then prick the pastry around the top of the pasties to allow steam to escape when they are baking.

5 Put the pasties on a baking sheet and brush with the remaining beaten egg. Bake in the oven for 20 minutes. Lower the oven to 180C/350F/Gas 4 and continue cooking for a further 10 minutes until golden brown. Serve hot, or leave to cool on a wire rack and serve cold.

Cook's Notes

 TIME
Preparation 30 minutes, cooking 30 minutes.

 FREEZING
Open freeze until solid, then pack in a rigid container, separating each one with foil. Seal, label and freeze for up to 3 months. To serve: reheat covered from frozen at 190C/375F/Gas 5 for 50 minutes.

 SERVING IDEAS
Serve the pasties hot or cold with a selection of relishes or pickled onions.

PREPARATION
To seal the edges of the pastry:

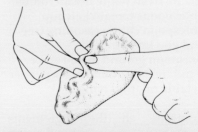

Press the pastry together over the top of the filling and then flute the edges to make the pasty shape.

●560 calories/2325 kj per pastry

Taverna tuna

SERVES 4

200 g/7 oz can tuna fish in oil,
   drained and flaked
250 g/9 oz cold cooked French
   beans, cut into 2.5 cm/1 inch
   lengths
½ Webb's or iceberg lettuce,
   separated into leaves
2 hard-boiled eggs, quartered
3 firm tomatoes, skinned and sliced
1 small onion, sliced into rings
8 black olives
8 green olives

GARLIC DRESSING
4 tablespoons olive oil (see
   Cook's tip)
2 tablespoons lemon juice
¼ teaspoon French mustard
½ teaspoon caster sugar
1 clove garlic, crushed
salt and freshly ground black pepper

1 Make the dressing: in a bowl
whisk together the oil, lemon juice,
mustard, sugar and garlic. Season
to taste with salt and pepper.
2 Put the tuna and beans in a bowl
and pour over half the dressing.
Toss until well coated.
3 Arrange the lettuce in a shallow
serving dish and spoon over the
tuna and beans. Arrange the eggs,
tomatoes, onion and olives over top.
Sprinkle over remaining dressing.

Cook's Notes

TIME
This salad takes about
35 minutes to prepare.

SERVING IDEAS
This makes a refreshing
starter for 6 people, or
will serve 4 as a supper or snack
either on its own or with crusty
French bread.

COOK'S TIP
Olive oil will give the
best flavour for this
dish but sunflower oil can be
used instead.

● 295 calories/1250 kj per portion

Rye bread zebras

MAKES 24

4 slices dark rye or pumpernickel
   bread (see Buying guide)
100 g/4 oz butter, at room
   temperature
2 hard-boiled eggs, finely chopped
few drops of yellow food colouring
   (optional)
salt and freshly ground black pepper
100 g/4 oz peeled prawns, defrosted
   if frozen, chopped
2 teaspoons tomato purée
squeeze of lemon juice
1 bunch watercress, finely chopped

1 Divide the butter equally between three bowls.

2 Add the eggs to one of the bowls with the food colouring, if using, then beat together until well blended. Season to taste with salt and pepper.

3 Add the prawns, tomato purée and lemon juice to another bowl of butter. Beat together and season to taste with salt and black pepper.

4 Add the watercress to remaining bowl and beat together well. Season to taste with salt and black pepper.

5 Spread prawn mixture on one slice of bread and cover with a second slice. Spread this with the egg mixture and cover with another slice of bread. Spread this with watercress mixture and top with the remaining slice of bread. Press the sandwich down firmly. Wrap in foil and refrigerate for at least 1 hour.

6 Using a sharp knife, cut sandwich into 6 slices lengthways and in 4 slices crossways to make 24 slices. Carefully place on a serving platter and serve (see Serving ideas).

Cook's Notes

 TIME
Preparation takes about 30 minutes, then allow 1 hour for chilling.

 BUYING GUIDE
Buy Danish or German rye or pumpernickel bread, sold in supermarkets wrapped in plastic or foil, which has a dense texture ideal for these sandwiches. To separate the slices without breaking them, use a palette knife and carefully slide it between slices to prise them apart.

ECONOMY
Use the left-over slices of bread to make sandwiches filled with curd cheese and chives.

 SERVING IDEAS
These rich-tasting sandwiches make a good accompaniment to a light soup such as tomato or onion. Alternatively, serve them as part of a party platter with canapés and other sandwiches.

●350 calories/450 kj per portion

Sausage and onion pies

SERVES 4
500 g/1 lb pork sausagemeat (see Buying guide)
8 sage sprigs, to garnish (optional)
vegetable oil, for greasing

FILLING
500 g/1 lb onions, quartered
salt
100 g/4 oz fresh white breadcrumbs
50 g/2 oz plain flour
25 g/1 oz margarine, softened
2 teaspoons dried sage
freshly ground black pepper

1 Heat the oven to 190C/375F/Gas 5. Brush 8 individual Yorkshire pudding tins with oil.

2 Prepare the filling: bring a pan of salted water to the boil and cook the onions for 5 minutes. Drain well and chop finely, then transfer to a bowl and add the breadcrumbs, flour, margarine and sage. Stir well to mix, then season to taste with salt and pepper.

3 Divide the sausagemeat into 8 pieces then, on a lightly floured board, roll each piece into a ball. Place a sausage ball in each tin and press down firmly with floured fingers, moulding the sausagemeat to the shape of the tins until the bases and sides are neatly lined.

4 Place 1 good tablespoon of the filling into each sausagemeat case and smooth over the top of the filling with a knife.

5 Bake just above the centre of the oven for 30-35 minutes or until golden brown and cooked through. Transfer to a warmed serving plate, garnish each pie with a sprig of sage, if liked, and serve at once.

Cook's Notes

TIME
Preparation takes about 30 minutes, cooking 30-35 minutes.

BUYING GUIDE
As the filling includes herbs, buy a plain sausagemeat for the cases.

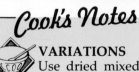

VARIATIONS
Use dried mixed herbs instead of sage. Top with a tomato slice 10 minutes before the end of cooking time.

SERVING IDEAS
Serve hot for a substantial supper dish with creamed potatoes topped with crushed potato crisps, and mixed peas and carrots.

These pies are also delicious cold with salad, and they make unusual picnic or lunch box food for children or adults.

●530 calories/2225 kj per portion

Devilled corn toasts

SERVES 4

8 streaky bacon rashers, rinds removed
50 g/2 oz margarine or butter
1 bunch spring onions, chopped
4 tablespoons single cream or top of the milk
100 g/4 oz Cheddar cheese, grated
4 slices medium-thick bread
2 × 200 g/7 oz cans sweetcorn, drained
2 tablespoons Worcestershire sauce
1 heaped teaspoon French mustard
salt and freshly ground black pepper
2 eggs, beaten

1 Heat the grill to moderate and grill the bacon until crisp. Drain on absorbent paper and keep warm.

2 Melt half the margarine in a small saucepan, add the spring onions and cook for 2-3 minutes until they are soft. Remove from the heat and stir in the cream and cheese. Return to the heat and cook gently, stirring, until the cheese has melted. !

3 Heat the grill to high and toast the bread.

4 Add the corn to the cheese and onion mixture with the Worcestershire sauce, mustard and salt and pepper to taste.

5 Add the beaten eggs to the corn mixture and cook, stirring, until the mixture has thickened.

6 Spread the remaining margarine over the toast and then divide the corn mixture between the slices. Top each with 2 bacon rashers and serve at once.

Cook's Notes

TIME
This tasty and filling snack takes about 10 minutes to prepare and cook.

VARIATIONS
Fry chopped mushrooms or green pepper with the spring onions and add to the mixture. For an even spicier taste, season the mixture with sweet paprika or cayenne.

WATCHPOINT
Cook the cream and cheese very gently; if the cream is allowed to come to boiling point it will separate.

●640 calories/2690 kj per portion

Fried sardine sandwiches

SERVES 4

100 g/4 oz sardines in oil, drained
2 large eggs, hard-boiled and
  chopped
2 tablespoons snipped chives or
  finely chopped spring onion tops
freshly ground black pepper
75 g/3 oz margarine or butter,
  softened
grated zest of 1 lemon
1 tablespoon lemon juice
generous pinch of sweet paprika
8 thin slices bread, crusts removed

1 Mash the sardines until smooth, then mix in the chopped eggs, chives and plenty of pepper.

2 Using a wooden spoon, beat the margarine in a separate bowl until light and creamy, then beat in the lemon zest, lemon juice and paprika.

3 Spread the bread slices on 1 side with the lemon-flavoured margarine. [!] Turn 4 of the slices over, and spread evenly with the sardine mixture. Top with the remaining 4 slices of bread, margarine side facing upwards.

4 Set a large frying-pan over fairly high heat and leave it for about 30 seconds to heat through (see Cook's tip). Put the sardine sandwiches into the pan and press them down gently with a fish slice.

5 Fry the sandwiches for about 3 minutes until golden brown, then carefully turn them over, using a fish slice, and cook for a further 3 minutes until golden brown. Serve at once.

Cook's Notes

 TIME
Preparation takes about 20 minutes, including hard-boiling the eggs. Frying the sandwiches takes about 6 minutes.

 VARIATION
Mix the mashed sardines with skinned, chopped tomatoes or peeled, diced cucumber instead of the egg.

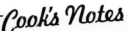 **WATCHPOINT**
Make sure you spread the margarine right to the edges of the slices of bread. This ensures an even, golden-brown finish.

 COOK'S TIP
No fat for frying is needed, as the sandwiches are spread on the outside with the margarine.

 SERVING IDEAS
These sandwiches are best eaten with a knife and fork.

Or cut each sandwich into 4 triangles with a sharp knife, and serve the triangles skewered with cocktail sticks and a garnish of tiny lemon wedges or lemon twists.

●350 calories/1475 kj per portion

Sausage and apple triangles

SERVES 4

350 g/12 oz sausagemeat
2 dessert apples, peeled and grated
215 g/7½ oz frozen puff pastry, defrosted
1 small onion, grated
salt and freshly ground black pepper
1 small egg, beaten, to glaze

1 Heat the oven to 220C/425F/Gas 7.
2 Roll out the pastry on a lightly floured surface to a 35 cm/14 inch square. Cut the pastry into four 17.5 cm/7 inch squares.
3 Put the sausagemeat in a bowl and then stir in the apples and onion.

Season to taste with salt and pepper.
4 Divide the sausagemeat mixture between the squares, spreading it diagonally over one half of each of the squares, leaving a 1 cm/½ inch border. Brush the edges of the pastry with beaten egg, then fold pastry over to form a triangle and enclose the filling. Press the edges firmly together to seal them, then knock up with the back of a knife. Brush the tops with beaten egg, then use a sharp knife to make 2 small slits to allow the steam to escape when baking.
5 Using a fish slice, carefully transfer the triangles to a dampened baking sheet. Bake in the oven for 20 minutes, then reduce the heat to 180C/350F/Gas 4 and bake for a further 25 minutes. Cover the pastry with foil during cooking if it shows signs of overbrowning. Serve hot or cold (see Serving ideas).

Cook's Notes

 TIME
Preparation takes 20 minutes and cooking 45 minutes.

 SERVING IDEAS
The triangles can be served hot as a supper dish accompanied by a green vegetable or baked beans, or they can be served cold for picnics and packed lunches.

 VARIATION
Add 1 teaspoon dried mixed herbs to the sausagemeat mixture for a more interesting flavour.

●525 calories/2200 kj per portion

144

Spicy club sandwich

MAKES 4

- 100 g/4 oz cooked chicken, chopped into bite-sized pieces
- 4 rashers back bacon, rinds removed
- 2 teaspoons mild curry powder
- 4 tablespoons mayonnaise
- 8 slices brown bread
- 4 slices white bread
- 50 g/2 oz butter, softened
- 4 small lettuce leaves
- 16 thin slices cucumber
- 2 tomatoes, sliced

1 Heat the grill to moderate. In a bowl, stir the curry powder into the mayonnaise and mix in the chicken. Lightly grill the bacon, drain well on absorbent paper and keep warm.

2 With a very sharp knife, remove the crusts from the bread and trim the slices to exactly the same size. Butter both sides of the white, and one side of the brown bread slices. Spread the chicken mixture equally over 4 slices of the brown bread. Top with the white bread slices.

3 Put a lettuce leaf and 4 slices of cucumber on each sandwich. Top with remaining brown bread slices.

4 Finally top each sandwich with tomato slices and a grilled bacon rasher.

Cook's Notes

TIME
Preparation takes about 30 minutes.

VARIATIONS
Cold cooked pork or canned tuna could be substituted for chicken.

SERVING IDEAS
You may find it easier to eat these double-decker sandwiches with a knife and fork.

●505 calories/2100 kj per portion

Stuffed leeks

SERVES 4

8 leeks, topped, tailed and thoroughly washed
salt
250 g/9 oz Gorgonzola cheese
1 egg, beaten
100 g/4 oz cooked ham, chopped
50 g/2 oz butter

1 Bring a pan of salted water to the boil and cook the leeks for about 20 minutes until they are tender.
2 Meanwhile, using a fork, mash the cheese in a bowl. Add the beaten egg and mix thoroughly together. Stir in the ham.
3 Heat the oven to 200C/400F/Gas 6.
4 Drain the leeks thoroughly and leave for about 10 minutes until cool enough to handle.
5 Push out the middle of the leeks to leave a tube (see Preparation). Fill the leeks with the cheese mixture, pressing the mixture in with a teaspoon handle.
6 Place the leeks in an ovenproof dish, dot with butter and bake for 15 minutes. Serve at once.

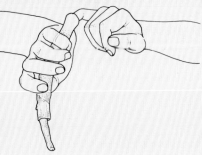

Saucy bacon rolls

SERVES 4

8 large rashers smoked back
  bacon, rinds removed
200 g/7 oz Red Leicester cheese,
  grated
2 tablespoons top of the milk or
  single cream
1 teaspoon made English mustard
½ teaspoon dried sage

1 Cover the grill rack with foil. Heat the grill to high.

2 Put the cheese in a mixing bowl and work in the milk or cream with a fork, to make a very thick paste. Mix in the mustard and sage until thoroughly blended.

3 Divide the cheese mixture equally between the bacon rashers, placing a portion on the wide end of each rasher. Roll the rashers up, starting at the wide end.

4 Lay the bacon rolls loose ends downwards on the heated grill rack and grill for 3-4 minutes on each side. Serve hot.

Cook's Notes

TIME
Total preparation and cooking time is 20 minutes.

BUYING GUIDE
Buy strong Cheddar cheese if Red Leicester is not available.

Unsmoked bacon can be used but will not give such a good flavour.

COOK'S TIPS
When grilling food, always make sure that both grill and rack are pre-heated. Covering the rack with foil stops the food falling into the pan during cooking.

The bacon rolls can be served on their own or on slices of French bread, toast or fried bread, with the melted cheese mixture spooned over.

●720 calories/3025 kj per portion

Avocado and shrimp toasties

SERVES 2

1 avocado
50 g/2 oz peeled shrimps
1 tablespoon horseradish sauce
2 tablespoons plus 2 teaspoons
   lemon juice
freshly ground black pepper
4 slices wholemeal bread
butter, for spreading
watercress, to garnish

1 Heat the grill to high.
2 Put the horseradish sauce and 2 teaspoons lemon juice in a small saucepan and heat gently. Add the shrimps and heat for a further 2-3 minutes. Season with pepper.
3 Meanwhile, peel, halve and stone the avocado, then slice the flesh thinly. Immediately sprinkle over the 2 tablespoons lemon juice to prevent the flesh discolouring.
4 Toast the bread on one side only, and butter the toasted sides.
5 Arrange slices of avocado on the toasted side of 2 of the slices of bread. Spread half the shrimp mixture over each and then put the other slices of bread on top, toasted side down.
6 Using 2 fish slices, lift the sandwiches into the grill pan and toast the top of each sandwich. Turn over and toast the bottom. Cut in half and serve at once, garnished with watercress.

Cook's Notes

 TIME
Preparation and toasting these sandwiches takes 15-20 minutes.

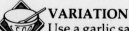 **VARIATION**
Use a garlic sausage and sweetcorn filling for these toasted sandwiches. For each sandwich, spread the buttered side with 2 tablespoons of sweetcorn relish. Arrange 50 g/2 oz sliced garlic sausage on top and sprinkle with 25 g/1 oz grated Cheddar or Stilton cheese.

●515 calories/2150 kj per portion

Creamed leek pastry

SERVES 4

750 g/1½ lb leeks, finely sliced

100 g/4 oz butter

350 g/12 oz frozen puff pastry,
  defrosted
1 small egg
salt
freshly grated nutmeg
3 tablespoons single cream
freshly ground black pepper

1 Heat the oven to 200C/400F/Gas 6.
2 Melt the butter in a large saucepan and add the leeks, stir and cover. Cook over very gentle heat for about 15 minutes, stirring occasionally until leeks are soft. [!]
3 Meanwhile, roll out the pastry on a lightly floured surface to a 33 × 23 cm/12 × 9 inch rectangle. Fold the pastry in half lengthways so that it measures 33 × 11½ cm/12 × 4½ inches. Lightly roll over the pastry to expel any air bubbles.

4 Press the edges of the pastry together well. Prick with a fork all over. Place the pastry strip on a dampened baking sheet and bake in the oven for 10 minutes.
5 Beat the egg lightly with a pinch of salt. Remove the pastry from the oven and brush with the egg, pressing the pastry down gently as you brush. Return to the oven for a

further 10 minutes until golden.
6 Add a little nutmeg to the cooked leeks, stir in the cream and season to taste with salt and pepper. Keep the leeks warm, but do not boil.
7 Carefully lift the pastry from the baking sheet and place on a serving plate (see Cook's tip). Spoon the leek mixture on top of the pastry and serve at once.

Cook's Notes

TIME
Preparation is about 10 minutes, cooking time 15 minutes for the leeks and 20 minutes for the pastry.

COOK'S TIP
If the pastry has risen unevenly, gently prick it to let the air escape and it will sink and become flat.

WATCHPOINT
Be careful not to let the leeks burn—cook them on the lowest possible heat.

SERVING IDEAS
Serve as a starter or a snack, with a tomato and cucumber salad.
  Make individual portions by cutting the long strip of pastry into four pieces before cooking.

VARIATIONS
Instead of leeks use grated or finely chopped carrots with ginger, or cabbage finely chopped with cinnamon added.

●630 calories/2625 kj per portion

Scrambled eggs and onions

SERVES 4

6 eggs
3 tablespoons milk
salt and freshly ground black pepper
50 g/2 oz margarine or butter
1 tablespoon vegetable oil
4 onions, thinly sliced
2 tablespoons snipped chives
8 slices of French bread,
 toasted, to serve

1 Beat the eggs in a bowl with the milk; season with salt and pepper.
2 Heat the margarine and oil in a frying-pan, add the onions and fry gently for about 20 minutes or until golden (see Cook's tips).
3 Add the egg mixture and cook over low heat, stirring constantly until the eggs are just set but not dry (see Cook's tips). Taste and adjust seasoning.
4 Pile on slices of French bread, sprinkle over chives and serve.

Cook's Notes

TIME
Preparation and cooking take 15 minutes.

VARIATIONS
Vary the flavour by adding a little freshly grated nutmeg or sweet paprika, or a mixture of chopped fresh herbs instead of the chives.

COOK'S TIPS
Take care not to let the onions become brown or they will impart a bitter flavour which will spoil the finished dish.
 Do not overcook the eggs—they taste best when left a little runny.

●270 calories/1125 kj per portion

150

Stuffed cucumber salad

SERVES 4

1 large cucumber, cut into 24 even
  slices (see Buying guide)
1 round lettuce, leaves separated
  (see Buying guide)
350 g/12 oz carrots, finely grated
3 tablespoons sultanas
small parsley sprigs and a few
  chopped walnuts, to garnish

FILLING

250 g/9 oz curd cheese
75 g/3 oz shelled walnuts, chopped
2 teaspoons finely chopped fresh
  parsley
2 teaspoons snipped fresh chives or
  finely chopped spring onion
½ teaspoon sweet paprika
salt and freshly ground black pepper

DRESSING

5 tablespoons vegetable oil
2 tablespoons white wine or cider
  vinegar
large pinch of mustard powder
pinch of caster sugar

1 Make the filling: put all the filling
ingredients in a bowl, season with
salt and pepper and mix well with a
fork.
2 Remove the seeds from each slice
of cucumber with an apple corer or a
small sharp knife. Season on both
sides with salt and pepper and set
out on a flat plate.
3 Divide the filling between the
cucumber slices, pressing it into the
central hole and piling it up on top.
4 Make the dressing: put all the
dressing ingredients in a small
screw-top jar, season with salt and
pepper then shake the jar well to mix
together.
5 Arrange the lettuce leaves on 4
individual plates and drizzle a
teaspoonful of the dressing over
each serving. Carefully transfer 6
cucumber slices to each plate,
arranging them in a ring.
6 Mix the grated carrots with the
sultanas in a bowl and add the
remaining dressing. Toss to coat
thoroughly, then pile into the centre
of the rings of stuffed cucumber
slices. Garnish 3 cucumber slices on
each plate with a parsley sprig and 3
slices with a few chopped walnuts.
Serve at once.

Cook's Notes

TIME
Preparation time is
about 45 minutes.

BUYING GUIDE
Choose a straight
cucumber so that it will
be easy to slice evenly.
  A curly, soft-leaved lettuce is
best for this recipe because it
gives an added attraction, but
any soft-leaved lettuce will do.

SERVING IDEAS
Serve the salad as a light
lunch or supper dish. It
could be accompanied by cold
sliced meat for a more filling
meal. The stuffed cucumber
slices, without the accompanying lettuce, can also be served as
a starter or with drinks.

VARIATION
Use chopped muscatel
raisins instead of
sultanas.

●410 calories/1730 kj per portion

Cheese and potato scones

MAKES 8-10 SCONES

100 g/4 oz mature Cheddar cheese, grated (see Cook's tip)
100 g/4 oz self-raising flour
2 teaspoons baking powder
¼ teaspoon salt
good pinch of mustard powder
25 g/1 oz butter, diced
100 g/4 oz potatoes, boiled, mashed and cooled
1 small egg
1 tablespoon milk
vegetable oil, for greasing

1 Heat the oven to 190C/375F/Gas 5. Grease a baking sheet.
2 Sift the flour, baking powder, salt and mustard into a bowl. Rub in the butter until the mixture resembles breadcrumbs, then stir in the cheese until thoroughly mixed.
3 Sieve the potatoes into the flour mixture and mix together with a round-bladed knife.

4 Beat the egg with the milk, then pour slowly into flour and potato mixture, adding just enough liquid to mix to a soft dough.
5 Turn the dough out on to a well-floured surface and knead lightly. ⚠ Roll out the dough to a thickness of 2 cm/¾ inch ⚠ and

cut into circles with a 5 cm/2 inch cutter. Knead remaining dough and roll out again to cut more circles.
6 Put the scones on to the prepared baking sheet and bake for about 15 minutes, until golden brown. Cool for a few minutes on a wire tray, then serve warm.

Cook's Notes

TIME
15 minutes preparation, 15 minutes cooking.

SERVING IDEAS
Serve buttered scones with soups or salads.

WATCHPOINTS
The dough is very soft to handle, so hands, work surface and rolling pin need to be well floured.
Do not roll out the dough too thinly: it does not rise very much during cooking, and if it is too thin the scones will be more like biscuits.

FREEZING
Cool the scones completely on a wire tray, pack in a polythene bag and seal, label and freeze for up to 6 months. To serve: defrost for 1-2 hours at room temperature, then warm through in a 180C/350F/Gas 4 oven for about 15 minutes.

COOK'S TIP
Use a strong-flavoured Cheddar cheese for these scones to really bring out the cheesy flavour.

● 125 calories/525 kj per scone

Aubergines on waffles

SERVES 4

2 large aubergines, cut into cubes
salt
2 tablespoons vegetable oil
300 ml/½ pint beef stock
4 teaspoons tomato purée
2 cloves garlic, crushed (optional)
½ teaspoon dark soft brown sugar
freshly ground black pepper
4 potato waffles
75 g/3 oz Cheddar cheese, grated
coriander sprigs or parsley, to garnish

1 Layer the aubergine cubes in a colander, sprinkling each layer with salt. Put a plate on top and weight down. Leave to drain for about 30 minutes to remove the bitter juices. Rinse under cold running water, pat dry with absorbent paper or a clean tea-towel and set aside.

2 Heat the oil in a large frying-pan, add the aubergines, stock, tomato purée, garlic, if using, and sugar. Season with salt and pepper.

3 Bring to the boil, then lower the heat, cover the pan and simmer for 8-10 minutes, stirring frequently, until the liquid is absorbed and the aubergines are tender.

4 Meanwhile, heat the grill to high and toast the waffles for 4 minutes on each side or fry as directed on the packet.

5 Place the waffles in a flameproof dish, pile the aubergine mixture on top and sprinkle over the grated cheese. Grill for 1-2 minutes (see Cook's tip).

6 Garnish waffles with coriander sprigs or parsley and serve at once.

Cheese crescents

MAKES 8

75 g/3 oz Leicester cheese, finely
   grated
400 g/13 oz frozen puff pastry,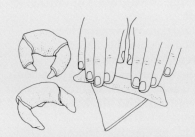
   defrosted
15 g/½ oz butter, melted
1 teaspoon celery salt
1 teaspoon mustard powder
freshly ground black pepper
1 egg, beaten, to glaze

1 Roll out the pastry on a floured surface to a 40 × 20 cm/16 × 8 inch rectangle. Brush with melted butter and sprinkle over the celery salt, mustard powder and a little freshly ground black pepper.
2 Sprinkle two-thirds of the rectangle with 50 g/2 oz of the cheese. Fold the plain one-third of pastry over the cheese and then fold over again (see Preparation). Seal the edges by pressing down firmly with a rolling pin.
3 Roll out to a 30 cm/12 inch square and cut into four 15 cm/6 inch squares. Cut each one in half diagonally to give 8 triangles. Shape into crescents (see Preparation), then refrigerate for 15 minutes.
4 Heat the oven to 220C/425F/Gas 7.
5 Place crescents on a dampened baking sheet. Brush with the beaten egg and sprinkle a little of the remaining grated cheese over each.
6 Bake in the oven for 15-20 minutes until golden brown and well risen. Serve warm or cold.

Cook's Notes

 TIME
These crescents are very easy to make, and they only take 10-15 minutes to prepare. Allow 15 minutes to chill the pastry, then baking time is 15-20 minutes.

 SERVING IDEAS
These crescents can be served warm, or left to cool on a wire rack and eaten cold. Serve without butter as a snack or with cheese and celery for a light supper.

 PREPARATION
To make and shape the cheese crescents:

1 *Fold the plain section of the pastry over the cheese, then fold over again. Seal edges by pressing down firmly with a rolling pin.*

2 *Roll up the pastry triangles from the widest part, finishing with the tip underneath. Gently curve the end to form a crescent shape.*

● 275 calories/1150 kj per crescent

Pissaladière

SERVES 4-6

215 g/7½ oz shortcrust pastry, defrosted if frozen (see Cook's tip)

FILLING
25 g/1 oz margarine or butter
2 onions, finely chopped
1 clove garlic, crushed (optional)
½ teaspoon dried mixed herbs
salt and freshly ground black pepper
egg white, for glazing (optional)
1 tablespoon French mustard
500 g/1 lb tomatoes, skinned and thickly sliced or 400 g/14 oz can tomatoes
50 g/2 oz Gruyère or Cheddar cheese, grated

TOPPING
50 g/2 oz can anchovies in olive oil, drained
5 black olives, halved and stoned

1 Heat the oven to 200C/400F/Gas 6.
2 Roll out the pastry on a floured board and use to line a 20 cm/8 inch flan tin or flan ring set on a baking sheet. Prick the pastry base all over with a fork. Line the pastry case with greaseproof paper or foil and weight it down with baking beans or rice. Bake blind in the oven for 10 minutes.
3 Meanwhile make the filling: melt the margarine in a frying-pan, add the onion and garlic, if using, and fry gently for 10 minutes until browned. Sprinkle over the dried mixed herbs and season with salt and pepper.
4 Remove the greaseproof or foil lining and the beans from the pastry case, and brush the inside of the pastry with beaten egg white, if liked. Return the flan tin to the oven and bake for a further 5 minutes. Remove from the oven and turn the heat down to 180C/350F/Gas 4.
5 Spread the mustard over the baked pastry base, then cover it with the onion mixture and then a layer of overlapping slices of tomato. Sprinkle over the cheese.
6 Arrange a lattice of anchovy fillets over the top of the cheese. Place half an olive, cut side down, in each diamond shape of the lattice.
7 Bake the pissaladière in the oven for about 30 minutes or until the pastry is crisp and golden brown.
8 Before serving, leave to stand for 5-10 minutes then remove from the tin and place on a serving plate. Serve warm.

Cook's Notes

TIME
Preparing and baking the pastry case takes 40 minutes. Baking the pissaladière takes 30 minutes, then allow 5-10 minutes cooling time.

DID YOU KNOW
Pissaladière originated in Nice, in the South of France, and the ingredients used in this rich, tasty flan are typical of that region.

SERVING IDEAS
Serve warm or cold as a starter or as a main dish with a fresh green salad.

COOK'S TIP
The pastry needs to be fairly thick for this recipe since the filling is so moist and tends to seep out.

● 365 calories/1525 kj per portion

Egg pâté

SERVES 4

200 g/7 oz full-fat soft cheese
4 hard-boiled eggs, shelled and
   roughly chopped (see Cook's tip)
1 tablespoon finely snipped chives
salt and freshly ground black pepper
stuffed olives, sliced, to garnish

1 Put the cheese into a bowl and beat until soft. Beat in the chopped eggs and chives and season well with salt and pepper.

2 Spoon into 4 individual dishes. Smooth the top of each with a palette knife, cover with cling film and refrigerate for 30 minutes.

3 To serve: garnish with the olive slices and serve at once.

Cook's Notes

 TIME
Preparation (including hard-boiling the eggs) takes about 30 minutes, but allow another 30 minutes for chilling.

VARIATIONS
Use a full-fat soft cheese flavoured with chives, herbs, garlic or crushed peppercorns, and omit the chives and/or the black pepper. For an extra 'tangy' flavour, add 1 teaspoon French mustard or Worcestershire sauce or a dash of Tabasco.

 COOK'S TIP
Hard-boiled eggs can be kept, unshelled, in a polythene bag in the refrigerator for 3-4 days.

 SERVING IDEAS
Serve as a dinner party starter or snack with toast fingers or bread rolls.

● 305 calories/1275 kj per portion

Parsley cheese bites

SERVES 4

75 g/3 oz full-fat soft cheese
100 g/4 oz Cheddar cheese, grated
50 g/2 oz Danish Blue cheese, at
    room temperature
freshly ground black pepper
4-5 tablespoons finely chopped
    fresh parsley
2-3 tablespoons plain flour

1 Work the cheeses together with a fork to form a smooth paste. Add pepper to taste.

2 Put the chopped parsley and flour on separate flat plates. Dip your hands in the flour, shaking off any excess, then shape the cheese mixture into 20 small balls, reflouring your hands as necessary. Roll each ball in chopped parsley.

3 Transfer to a serving plate and refrigerate for 30 minutes before serving. Serve chilled.

Oriental citrus salad

SERVES 4
1 grapefruit
2 oranges
½ cucumber, sliced
1 onion, sliced into rings
**225 g/8 oz can water chestnuts,
  drained and sliced (see
  Variation)**
**100 g/4 oz fresh spinach, washed
  and thoroughly dried**
100 g/4 oz Edam cheese, sliced
1 tablespoon white wine vinegar
2 tablespoons sugar
2 teaspoons soy sauce
**few drops hot pepper sauce or
  Tabasco**

1 Peel the grapefruit and oranges
and divide into segments over a
bowl to catch any juice. Put the fruit
into a large bowl and mix in the
cucumber, onion rings, and the
water chestnuts.
2 Arrange spinach on a serving
platter, then place the cheese in
overlapping slices at the edge.
3 Put the vinegar, sugar, soy sauce
and hot pepper sauce into the bowl
with the fruit juices and whisk with
a fork until well blended. Pour over
the grapefruit mixture and toss.
4 Spoon the tossed salad on to the
spinach. Refrigerate for 30 minutes,
then serve chilled.

Cook's Notes

TIME
Preparation of this
salad takes 20 minutes.

VARIATION
If water chestnuts are
unavailable, use 100 g/
4 oz sliced button mushrooms
instead.

SERVING IDEAS
Serve this colourful
salad with wholemeal
bread and butter for a light
vegetarian lunch. It also makes
an attractive addition to a
summer barbecue.

●180 calories/750 kj per portion

Melted Mozzarella sandwiches

SERVES 4
8 large slices white bread
50 g/2 oz butter, softened
freshly ground black pepper
Worcestershire sauce
100 g/4 oz Mozzarella cheese (see Buying guide)
3 eggs, beaten
vegetable oil, for frying
parsley sprigs, to garnish

1 Spread the bread with the butter and cut off the crusts (see Cook's tip) with a sharp knife. ⚠ Season 4 of the bread slices with pepper and a few drops of Worcestershire sauce.

2 Cut the Mozzarella into thin slices and arrange them in a single layer on the seasoned bread, leaving a 5 mm/¼ inch margin all round the edge of the bread.

3 Top with the remaining 4 bread slices. Press the edges firmly together.

4 Put beaten eggs on a plate and dip in each sandwich to coat thoroughly all over. Make sure that the edges are well covered with egg so that they are sealed.

5 Heat the oven to 110C/225F/Gas ¼. Pour enough oil into a large frying-pan to come to a depth of 5 mm/¼ inch. Heat gently until a bread crust sizzles and turns golden brown when dropped into the oil.

6 Fry the sandwiches 2 at a time for 3-4 minutes on each side until golden brown.

7 Drain very thoroughly on absorbent paper. Keep warm in the oven while frying the remaining sandwiches. Serve at once, garnished with parsley sprigs.

Cook's Notes

 TIME
The sandwiches take about 15 minutes to prepare and cook.

DID YOU KNOW
In Italy these sandwiches are called Mozzarella in *carrozza* (a small covered carriage).

 **COOK'S TIP**
Use a little of the removed bread crust to test the temperature of the oil.

 WATCHPOINT
It is important that the bread slices are exactly the same size so that they can be sealed neatly.

BUYING GUIDE
Mozzarella cheese has outstanding melting qualities. If you can, buy an individually packed Mozzarella cheese from an Italian delicatessen; a single cheese will weigh about 100 g/4 oz.

●365 calories/1525 kj per portion

Nutty savoury scones

MAKES 6
275 g/10 oz self-raising flour
1 teaspoon baking powder
freshly ground black pepper
50 g/2 oz margarine, diced
25 g/1 oz salted peanuts, chopped
1 egg, beaten
6-8 tablespoons milk
vegetable oil, for greasing

TOPPING
3 tablespoons smooth peanut butter
50 g/2 oz full-fat soft cheese
50 g/2 oz Danish Blue cheese, crumbled
1 tablespoon single cream
salt
mustard and cress, to garnish

1 Heat the oven to 220C/425F/Gas 7. Lightly grease a baking sheet.

2 Sift the flour and baking powder into a bowl and season with pepper. Add the margarine and rub it in with your fingertips until the mixture resembles fine breadcrumbs.
3 Stir in the chopped peanuts and beaten egg, and enough milk to mix to a soft dough.
4 Roll out the dough on a lightly floured surface until 2 cm/¾ inch thick and cut into rounds with a 7.5 cm/3 inch biscuit cutter. Roll out the trimmings and cut out more rounds

until there are 6 of them altogether.
5 Place the scones on the baking sheet and bake for 15-20 minutes.
6 Meanwhile, make the topping: put the peanut butter and cheeses into a bowl. Add the cream and mix with a fork until evenly blended. Season lightly with salt and pepper.
7 Remove the cooked scones from oven, carefully cut in half, then spread with the topping. Serve hot, garnished with a few sprigs of mustard and cress.

Melon bowl salads

SERVES 4

2 ogen melons (see Buying guide)
**175 g/6 oz Mozzarella cheese, cut
  into 1 cm/½ inch cubes (see
  Variation)**
6 tomatoes, skinned and quartered
1 tablespoon snipped chives
1 tablespoon chopped basil or mint

DRESSING
2 tablespoons wine vinegar
6 tablespoons vegetable or olive oil
salt and freshly ground black pepper

1 Cut melons in half crossways or
vandyke them (see Serving ideas).
Discard the seeds and scoop out the
flesh with a melon baller or slice
into small cubes with a sharp knife.
Place the melon balls in a large bowl.

Wrap melon shells tightly in cling
film and refrigerate until required.
2 Add the cheese, tomatoes and
herbs to the melon balls.
3 Make the dressing: put dressing
ingredients into a screw-top jar with
salt and pepper to taste and shake

well to mix. Pour the dressing over
the salad and then toss thoroughly
(see Cook's tip).
4 Cut a thin slice from the base of
each melon shell so they stand
upright. Divide the salad between
the melon shells and serve at once.

Cook's Notes

 TIME
This salad takes only
20 minutes to prepare.

 COOK'S TIP
Chilling helps the fla-
vours to combine so, if
wished, cover the salad tightly
and refrigerate for 2 hours.

 BUYING GUIDE
If ogen melons are not
available, use Gallia or
cantaloupe or 2 small honeydew melons.

 SERVING IDEAS
Serve with hot garlic
bread for a light lunch.
To vandyke the melons: cut in a
zig-zag shape all round.

 VARIATION
For a more piquant
salad, use 175 g/6 oz
Feta cheese in place of the Mozzarella cheese but crumble it
into the bowl instead of cutting
into cubes.

●370 calories/1550 kj per portion

Savoury shortbread

MAKES 8 SLICES

150 g/5 oz plain flour
25 g/1 oz ground rice
good pinch of freshly grated
  nutmeg
good pinch of mustard powder
good pinch of salt
100 g/4 oz margarine or butter
100 g/4 oz Cheddar cheese, finely
  grated
1 tablespoon tomato ketchup

1 Heat the oven to 150C/300F/Gas 2.
Lightly flour an 18 cm/7 inch loose-
bottomed flan tin.

2 In a bowl, mix together the flour,
ground rice, nutmeg, mustard and
salt. Cut the margarine into 1 cm/
½ inch cubes and rub it in until
the mixture resembles fine
breadcrumbs. Stir in the cheese and
tomato ketchup and blend until well
mixed and evenly coloured.
3 With floured hands, gather the
dough together in a ball and place in
the prepared tin. Press down firmly
until the mixture is spread evenly
over the tin and then, using a
floured fork, press the prongs firmly
around the edge. Prick all over the
pastry with the fork.
4 Bake just below the centre of the
oven for about 1 hour or until golden
brown.
5 Cut the shortbread into 8 portions
while hot, then leave to cool in tin.

Cook's Notes

 TIME
Preparation 15 minutes,
cooking 1 hour.

 SERVING IDEAS
Serve with hot soups or
salads instead of bread.

 VARIATIONS
Add 1-2 teaspoons
finely chopped fresh
herbs and bind the mixture
together with cream instead of
tomato ketchup. Or use a
flavoured Cheddar cheese such
as onion and chive.

●220 calories/925 kj per slice

162

Fruit and cheese kebabs

SERVES 4

50 g/2 oz curd cheese
25 g/1 oz seedless raisins, chopped
2 tablespoons walnuts or unsalted peanuts, finely chopped
50 g/2 oz Danish blue cheese
50 g/2 oz smoked cheese
50 g/2 oz Leicester or Red Cheshire cheese
1 large red-skinned dessert apple
juice of 1 lemon
300 g/11 oz can mandarin orange segments, well drained, or 2 fresh mandarin oranges, peeled and divided into segments
225 g/8 oz can pineapple chunks, well drained
100 g/4 oz black or green grapes, washed and dried
6 lettuce leaves, shredded, to serve

1 Put the curd cheese into a bowl with the raisins and mix well. Roll into 8 small even-sized balls.

2 Spread the chopped nuts out on a flat plate and roll the balls in them. Transfer to a plate and refrigerate while you prepare the other ingredients.

3 Cut the Danish blue cheese into 8 even-sized cubes. Repeat with both the smoked cheese and the Leicester cheese.

4 Quarter and core the apple, but do not peel it. Cut in even sized slices and immediately squeeze the lemon juice over them to prevent discoloration.

5 On 8 individual skewers, spear 1 curd cheese ball and 1 cube each of Danish blue, smoked and Leicester cheeses, interspersed with apple slices, mandarin orange segments, pineapple chunks and grapes. Serve 2 skewers per person on a bed of shredded lettuce.

Cook's Notes

 TIME
Total preparation time is about 20 minutes.

SERVING IDEAS
These kebabs make an interesting and refreshing snack or an unusual, fresh-tasting dinner party starter. Slices of brown bread and butter go well with them, or they can be served inside wholemeal pitta bread.

●355 calories/1450 kj per kebab

VARIATIONS
You can vary the ingredients according to the cheese, nuts and fruit you prefer and have available; you can also add salad ingredients such as red or green pepper, chunks of cucumber, radishes or tiny tomatoes.

 ECONOMY
If you have any fruit left over, tip it into a bowl and add a can of guavas for a quick fruit salad.

Spinach and Brie puffs

SERVES 4

225 g/8 oz frozen spinach, defrosted
   and well drained (see Cook's tip)
50 g/2 oz Brie, thinly sliced (see
   Buying guide)
1 egg, beaten
¼ teaspoon freshly grated nutmeg
salt and freshly ground black pepper
215 g/7½ oz frozen puff pastry,
   defrosted
15 g/½ oz grated Parmesan cheese

Cook's Notes

 TIME
The puffs take about 20 minutes to prepare and 10 minutes to cook.

 SERVING IDEAS
Make the puffs smaller (cut 7.5 cm/3 inch squares) for an unusual starter or snack to serve with drinks.

COOK'S TIP
Put the spinach into a colander or sieve and drain thoroughly, pressing the spinach with a large spoon or a saucer to extract as much moisture as possible.

 BUYING GUIDE
Look for Brie that is not too ripe. If it is quite soft, put it in the freezer or freezing compartment of the refrigerator for about 30 minutes before making the puffs.

● 320 calories/1350 kj per puff

1 Heat the oven to 220C/425F/Gas 7.
2 Put the spinach in a bowl, stir in half the beaten egg and the nutmeg. Season to taste with salt and pepper.
3 Roll out the pastry on a lightly floured surface. Trim to a 30 cm/12 inch square, then cut into four 15 cm/6 inch squares.
4 Divide the spinach equally between the squares, spreading it diagonally over one-half of each and leaving a 1 cm/½ inch border. Top the squares with Brie slices, dividing them equally between the 4 squares.
5 Brush the edges of the pastry with beaten egg, then fold the pastry over to form a triangle and enclose the filling. Press the edges firmly together to seal them, then knock up with a knife and flute. Brush the tops with beaten egg, then use a sharp knife to make 2 small slits to allow the steam to escape. Sprinkle over the Parmesan cheese.
6 Dampen a baking sheet and carefully transfer the triangles to it.
7 Bake in the oven for about 10 minutes, until the pastry is golden. Serve the puffs hot or cold.

Tortellini with tomato sauce

SERVES 4-6
500 g/1 lb tortellini (see Buying guide)
salt
4 slices processed cheese (see For children)

SAUCE
400 g/14 oz can tomatoes
1 onion, chopped
few sprigs parsley
salt
25 g/1 oz margarine
25 g/1 oz plain flour
1 teaspoon tomato purée
1 teaspoon clear honey
freshly ground black pepper

1 Make sauce: work the tomatoes, onion and the parsley sprigs in a blender and add ½ teaspoon salt.
2 Melt the margarine in a saucepan, sprinkle in the flour and stir over low heat for 1-2 minutes until straw-coloured. Gradually stir in the puréed mixture, then add tomato purée and honey. Season to taste with salt and pepper. Simmer very gently for 20 minutes, until the sauce is thick and quite smooth.
3 Meanwhile, bring a large pan of salted water to the boil and cook the tortellini for 3-4 minutes if fresh (or according to packet instructions, if dried). Meanwhile, heat the grill to high. Drain thoroughly and divide between 4 individual flameproof dishes. Pour over the tomato sauce and place a cheese slice on top. Place the dishes under the grill for about 3 minutes, until cheese is melted. Serve at once.

Cook's Notes

 TIME
Preparing and cooking take only 45 minutes.

 BUYING GUIDE
Tortellini are small circles of stuffed pasta available either fresh or dried. Fresh tortellini are sold loose or packed in plastic boxes from delicatessens and some large supermarkets. They can be either plain or green and stuffed with either a meat or cheese filling. Dried varieties are sold in packets at most supermarkets. All are suitable for this dish.

FOR CHILDREN
Use animal-shaped or other fancy biscuit cutters to cut cheese slices into fun shapes. But watch the grilling – if the cheese melts too much the cheese figures will lose their distinctive shapes.

●380 calories/1575 kj per portion

Pulse-filled pittas

SERVES 4

250 g/9 oz split red lentils
40 g/1½ oz margarine or butter
1 onion, finely chopped
100 g/4 oz button mushrooms,
  thinly sliced
2 teaspoons ground cumin
450 ml/16 fl oz chicken or ham stock
2 tablespoons lemon juice
1 tablespoon finely chopped fresh
  parsley
salt and freshly ground black pepper
4 white or brown pitta breads
4 tomatoes, thinly sliced

1 Melt the margarine in a saucepan. Add the onion and fry gently for 3-4 minutes until soft but not coloured. Add the mushrooms and cumin and fry for a further 2 minutes, stirring.

2 Add the lentils and stock to the pan and bring to the boil, then turn down the heat to very low. Cover and simmer for 20-30 minutes, stirring occasionally until the lentils are soft and the liquid has been absorbed.

3 Heat the grill to high.

4 Add the lemon juice and parsley and season to taste with salt and pepper. Keep warm over low heat, stirring occasionally until the mixture is really thick.

5 Dampen the pitta breads by sprinkling them all over with cold water, then toast them (see Cook's tip) for 2-3 minutes on each side, until just crisp. Cut them in half, horizontally, and ease open with a round-bladed knife. Divide the lentil mixture between the pitta 'pockets' and slip a few tomato slices into each one. Serve at once.

Cook's Notes

TIME
Total preparation and cooking time for this wholefood snack is about 50 minutes.

SERVING IDEAS
Fold a paper napkin around each filled pitta, so that it can be eaten in the hand.

Serve with a Greek-style salad made with shredded lettuce or white cabbage, sliced tomatoes, cucumber and a few black olives. Crumbled or cubed Greek Feta cheese makes a tasty topping to this salad; or Caerphilly can be used as an alternative if Feta is difficult to obtain.

COOK'S TIP
Dampening the pitta breads keeps them soft and prevents them becoming dry and cracked when toasted. If cut in half, they can be toasted in an automatic 'pop-up' toaster.

●495 calories/2075 kj per portion

Stilton eggs

SERVES 4

100 g/4 oz Stilton cheese, rind removed
150 ml/¼ pint double cream
freshly ground black pepper
4 eggs
fresh tarragon leaves, to garnish (optional)

1 Heat the oven to 200C/400F/Gas 6.
2 Crumble the cheese into a bowl, add the cream and beat until smooth. Season the mixture to taste with freshly ground black pepper.
3 Divide mixture between 4 individual ramekin dishes. Break an egg into each. Place on a baking sheet and bake eggs in the oven for 15-20 minutes until the mixture is bubbling and eggs are just set.
4 Garnish with 2-3 tarragon leaves, if using, and serve at once while still piping hot (see Serving ideas).

Cook's Notes

 TIME
Preparation and cooking take 30 minutes.

 VARIATION
Instead of cooking in dishes, remove some of flesh from jacket-baked potatoes, spoon the mixture into them and bake as above.

SERVING IDEAS
Served with slices of Melba toast, these eggs make a delicious dinner party starter. Alternatively, serve them with bread and butter and glasses of port as an unusual light supper dish.

●360 calories/1500 kj per portion

Scotch woodcock

SERVES 4

50 g/2 oz can anchovies, drained
   and halved lengthways
4 tablespoons milk
6 eggs
salt and freshly ground black pepper
4 large slices bread, crusts removed
50 g/2 oz margarine or butter
strips of pimiento and parsley
   sprigs, to garnish

1 Heat the oven to 110C/225F/
Gas ¼. Put the anchovies in a shallow dish and cover them with half
the milk. Set aside for 20 minutes.
2 Break the eggs into a bowl, add
remaining milk and season to taste
with salt and pepper. Whisk lightly.
3 Drain the anchovies and pat dry
with absorbent paper.
4 Toast the bread lightly on both
sides, spread with half the margarine and keep warm in the oven.

5 Melt the remaining margarine in a
large saucepan. Pour in the whisked
eggs. Stir over moderate heat with a
wooden spoon until the egg is just
set in soft, creamy flakes. ⟨!⟩

6 Immediately pile the scrambled
egg on to the slices of toast, then
arrange the anchovies in a lattice
pattern on top. Serve at once,
garnished with parsley sprigs.

Cook's Notes

TIME
Preparation and cooking take about 35
minutes.

PREPARATION
Halve the anchovies
with a small sharp knife.

WATCHPOINT
When scrambling eggs,
keep the heat moderate
or they will set too quickly at the
base, like an omelette. Keep the
egg moving by stirring gently
and serve immediately the
surface looks creamy. The egg
will continue to cook for a few
seconds after the pan is
removed from the heat.

SERVING IDEAS
For a change, cut the
bread slices into circles
or other shapes and then
garnish the scrambled egg on
some of them with pimiento
strips instead of the anchovies
and parsley sprigs.

DID YOU KNOW
Scotch woodcock is an
English 'savoury', a
dish that was traditionally eaten
at the end of a meal. Nowadays,
when fewer courses are eaten
and meals tend to be less formal,
savouries are more often eaten
as supper or snack dishes.

●285 calories/1200 kj per portion

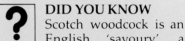

Fruit'n'nut snacks

SERVES 4
4 slices white bread
4 slices wholemeal or granary bread
40 g/1½ oz soft tub margarine
1-2 tablespoons chocolate spread
50 g/2 oz stoned dates, chopped
50 g/2 oz fresh skinned peanuts, chopped
1 dessert apple

1 Put the margarine in a bowl and stir in the chocolate spread, dates and peanuts. Core and finely chop the apple, leaving the skin on, then add it to the bowl. Mix well to combine all the ingredients.

2 If wished, remove crusts from bread. Divide the mixture equally between the slices of white bread, spread it on evenly, then cover with the brown slices.

3 Cut each of the sandwiches into 4 triangles, then arrange them on a serving plate – half with the brown bread uppermost and half with the white bread on top.

Cook's Notes

TIME
These sandwiches take 20 minutes to prepare.

FOR CHILDREN
For children's parties, extra margarine with chocolate spread mixed into it can be piped in small swirls on each sandwich and decorated with peanuts or dates.

●350 calories/1475 kj per portion

Cheese and chicken pockets

SERVES 4

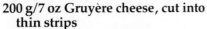 200 g/7 oz Gruyère cheese, cut into
thin strips
 250 g/9 oz cooked chicken, thinly
sliced (see Buying guide)
4 pitta breads
1 small green pepper, deseeded and
sliced into thin rings
2 large firm tomatoes, thinly sliced
salt and freshly ground black pepper
3 tablespoons mango chutney

1 Heat the oven to 200C/400F/Gas 6.
Cut out 8 squares of foil each large
enough to enclose half a pitta.
2 Cut each pitta bread in half
crossways and ease the pockets open
with a knife, taking care not to pierce
the sides of the bread.
3 Divide the ingredients for the
filling into 8, then hold each pitta
pocket open with one hand and,
with the other, layer the ingredients
into the pockets in the following
order: green pepper, cheese, tomato
and chicken. ⚠ Sprinkle each layer
with a little salt and pepper, then
spread the chicken with chutney.

4 Place each filled pocket, chicken
layer uppermost, on a square of foil,
and wrap securely in a parcel. Put the
parcels on 1 or 2 baking sheets, and
heat through in the oven for about 20
minutes. Serve at once.

Cook's Notes

 TIME
Preparation takes about
30 minutes. Heating
through takes 20 minutes.

SERVING IDEAS
These tasty chicken
pockets can be heated
on a barbecue instead of in the
oven. They are best eaten with
fingers so provide each person
with just a plate and a napkin.

 VARIATIONS
Try using cooked lamb,
beef, ham or turkey in-
stead of chicken. Another good
melting cheese, such as
Mozzarella, can be used instead
of the Gruyère.

 WATCHPOINT
The order in which the
pittas are filled is
important. If tomato is put next
to the bread, the bread will
become soggy.

BUYING GUIDE
Sliced, pressed rolled
chicken, available from
supermarkets and delicatessens, is ideal for this recipe and
saves preparation time.

●570 calories/2400 kj per portion

Tomato-nested eggs

SERVES 4

400 g/14 oz can tomatoes
1 tablespoon dried onion flakes
¼ teaspoon chilli seasoning
pinch of cayenne pepper
salt
120 g/4¼ oz packet instant potato
25 g/1 oz margarine or butter,
   softened
freshly ground black pepper
4 eggs
50 g/2 oz Cheddar cheese, finely
   grated
margarine or butter, for greasing

1 Heat the oven to 130C/250F/Gas½.
Grease 4 individual soufflé dishes.
2 Put the tomatoes with their juice
into a saucepan, then add the onion
flakes, chilli seasoning, cayenne
pepper and salt to taste. Bring to the
boil, stirring and breaking up the
tomatoes with a wooden spoon.
Lower the heat and simmer,
uncovered, for about 15 minutes,
until the liquid is reduced and the
mixture has thickened. !
3 Make up the instant potato
according to packet instructions.
Beat in the margarine, then season
to taste with salt and pepper.
4 Spoon a ring of potato around the
edge of each greased soufflé dish,
then fork the top to make an
attractive pattern. Spread the
tomato mixture evenly over the
bottom of the dishes and make a
shallow depression in each one.
Keep hot in the oven.
5 Heat the grill to high.
6 Meanwhile, in a large frying-pan,
heat water to a depth of 2.5 cm/1
inch until it barely simmers.
! Break each egg into a cup or small
bowl and carefully slip the eggs into
the pan of water. Poach very gently
for about 2 minutes until just set,
basting the tops of the eggs with hot
water once or twice.
7 Remove the eggs from the pan
with a slotted spoon and carefully
place in the prepared soufflé dishes.
Season lightly with salt and pepper,
then sprinkle the grated cheese over
the top. Place under the grill for 1-2
minutes, until the cheese has
melted. Serve at once.

Cook's Notes

TIME
Preparation and cooking
take about 35 minutes.

WATCHPOINTS
The tomato mixture
must be thick, not
liquid, or the egg whites will
mix into it and not set properly.
   The heat should be low
enough for there to be just the
slightest trace of simmering
bubbles on the base of the pan.

VARIATIONS
Top the nested eggs
with a little tomato
purée. Gruyère cheese goes well
with eggs and could be used
instead of Cheddar.

●305 calories/1275 kj per portion

Milky snacks

SERVES 4
4 ripe bananas
4 eggs
4 teaspoons clear honey
juice of 2 small oranges
600 ml/1 pint milk
½ teaspoon ground cinnamon

1 Put the bananas, eggs and honey in a blender and work until smooth (see Cook's tip).
2 Add the orange juice, milk and cinnamon and blend again.
3 Pour into 4 tall glasses and serve.

Cheese and sultana roll-ups

SERVES 4

175 g/6 oz curd cheese
100 g/4 oz Cheddar cheese, finely grated
50 g/2 oz sultanas
pinch of freshly grated nutmeg
salt and freshly ground black pepper
12 large slices day-old brown bread, crusts removed (see Buying guide)
50 g/2 oz butter
2 tablespoons vegetable oil
small sprigs of parsley, to garnish (optional)

1 Heat the oven to 110C/225F/Gas ¼.
2 Put the curd cheese in a bowl and stir in the Cheddar cheese, sultanas and grated nutmeg. Season to taste with salt and ground black pepper.
3 Using a rolling pin, roll the bread slices as thinly as possible. Spread the slices with the cheese mixture, leaving a 1 cm/½ inch border on one side. Turn each slice of bread so that the uncovered border is away from you, then very carefully roll up the slice towards the border.
4 Melt half the butter and oil in a large frying-pan. When the foaming subsides, lay 6 of the rolls in the pan, seam side down and fry over moderate heat for about 1 minute. Continue to fry for 4-5 minutes, turning with a fish slice until golden brown all over. ⚠
5 Remove the rolls from the pan using a fish slice and drain on absorbent paper. Keep them warm while frying the remaining rolls in the remaining butter and oil.
6 Garnish each roll with a parsley sprig, if wished. Transfer to a serving plate and serve at once.

Herby omelette slices

SERVES 4

6 eggs
3 tablespoons milk
salt and freshly ground black pepper
25 g/1 oz butter
**1 round lettuce, separated into
    leaves**
4 large tomatoes, thinly sliced

FILLING
**4 tablespoons thick bottled
    mayonnaise**
**4 tablespoons finely chopped fresh
    parsley**
3 tablespoons snipped chives
**4½ teaspoons finely chopped fresh
    chervil (see Variation)**
**1 tablespoon finely chopped fresh
    coriander**

DRESSING
150 ml/¼ pint soured cream
1 tablespoon lemon juice
½ teaspoon caster sugar
¼ teaspoon sweet paprika

1 Put 2 of the eggs in a bowl with 1 tablespoon of the milk and season with salt and pepper to taste. Beat together lightly with a fork.

Cook's Notes

TIME
Preparation and cooking takes 50-60 minutes, chilling 1-2 hours.

SERVING IDEAS
For a buffet dish, serve the salad on a large platter with brown bread and butter and dry white wine.

VARIATION
Vary the herbs for the filling according to what is available. Fresh dill, mint and basil are all equally suitable alternatives and any combination of them can be used for the omelette.

●365 calories/1525 kj per portion

2 Melt one-third of the butter in a 20 cm/8 inch frying-pan over moderate heat. When it sizzles pour in the eggs and cook for about 1½ minutes, lifting the edges with a palette knife and tilting the pan so that the unset egg flows underneath. When the omelette is golden brown on the underside and set but still soft on top, slide it out of pan on to a large plate.

3 Make 2 more omelettes in the same way, using the remaining eggs, milk and butter. Pile the omelettes, one on top of the other, on the plate and leave them to cool completely.

4 Meanwhile, make the filling: put the mayonnaise into a bowl, mix in the herbs and season to taste with salt and pepper.

5 Spread a quarter of the herb mixture over 1 omelette. Roll up the omelette and lay it, with the join underneath, on a large plate. Repeat with the remaining 2 omelettes, then cover and refrigerate for 1-2 hours.

6 Mix together the dressing ingredients in a bowl, adding salt and pepper to taste. Stir in the remaining quarter of herb mixture and refrigerate until needed.

7 To serve: arrange lettuce leaves around the edge of a large serving plate. Place a ring of overlapping tomato slices on top.

8 Cut the rolled omelettes across into 2 cm/¾ inch slices and put them, cut sides up, within the ring of tomatoes. Serve the omelette slices with the soured cream dressing handed separately in a serving jug (see Serving ideas).

Pipérade

SERVES 4

250 g/9 oz red or green peppers,
   deseeded and sliced
50 g/2 oz butter
1 onion, finely chopped
2 cloves garlic, crushed (optional)
225 g/8 oz can tomatoes, drained
   and chopped
pinch of cayenne
salt and freshly ground black pepper
6 eggs
2 tablespoons milk

1 Melt the butter in a heavy-based frying-pan. Add the onion and the garlic, if using, and fry gently for 5 minutes until it is just soft and lightly coloured.

2 Add the peppers, tomatoes and cayenne and season with salt and pepper to taste. Simmer, stirring occasionally, for about 20 minutes, or until the pepper and tomato mixture is thick.

3 Lightly beat the eggs with the milk and a little salt and pepper.

Pour into the pan and cook for 2-3 minutes, stirring with a wooden spatula until the eggs are just set but not dry. Transfer the pipérade to a warmed serving dish and serve at once while piping hot.

Cook's Notes

 TIME
Preparing and cooking the pipérade take a total of about 35 minutes.

 COOK'S TIP
Prepare the red pepper and tomato mixture in advance, then reheat and use as a filling for omelettes or spoon on to scrambled eggs.

 WATCHPOINT
The mixture must be very thick, otherwise the finished dish will be watery.

 VARIATION
For a more substantial dish, add 50 g/2 oz diced cooked ham to the pan and heat through before adding the eggs in stage 3.

 DID YOU KNOW
This garlicky tomato, pepper and onion egg dish originated in the Basque region of south-western France where it is traditionally served with cold sliced ham.

● 235 calories/975 kj per portion

Sweetcorn waffles

MAKES 8-10 WAFFLES

**200 g/7 oz canned sweetcorn,
  drained**
175 g/6 oz plain flour
1 tablespoon baking powder
2 eggs, separated
300 ml/½ pint milk
75 g/3 oz butter, melted
salt and freshly ground black pepper
vegetable oil, for greasing

1 Sift the flour and baking powder into a bowl and make a well in the centre. Add the egg yolks and beat thoroughly, gradually working the dry ingredients into the centre. Add the milk and melted butter and beat until smooth. Stir in the sweetcorn and season the mixture to taste with salt and pepper.
2 In a clean, dry bowl, whisk the egg whites until standing in stiff peaks, then, using a metal spoon, carefully fold into the batter.

3 Lightly grease a waffle iron with oil (see Cook's tips) and set over high heat for about 2 minutes until it is hot, turning occasionally so that both plates are heated. Lower the heat to moderate. Spoon a little batter into the heated waffle iron. Close the lid and cook for 30-60 seconds, then turn the waffle iron over and cook for a further 30-60 seconds until the sweetcorn waffle is a light golden brown on both sides (see Cook's tips).
4 Open the lid and lift out waffle with a palette knife. Serve at once (see Cook's tips).

Cook's Notes

 TIME
Preparation 10 minutes, cooking 10 minutes.

 COOK'S TIPS
If you do not have a waffle iron, a lightly oiled girdle or frying-pan may be used instead. Simply drop tablespoons of the sweetcorn mixture on to the girdle or pan and cook for 1-2 minutes, turning the waffles once.

Use the first waffle as a test one to make sure the heat is high enough and the quantity of batter is correct. The number of waffles will depend on the size and shape of the waffle iron used; some types cook 1 waffle at a time, others cook several waffles together.

Waffles are at their best when served immediately but, if they are to be kept hot for a short time, place in a single layer on a wire rack in a low oven. Do not pile them on top of each other or they will become soft.

SERVING IDEAS
These waffles are delicious served for breakfast with grilled bacon.

●210 calories/875 kj per waffle

Union snack

MAKES 4

4 large round soft rolls

75 g/3 oz margarine or butter, softened

75 g/3 oz Red Leicester cheese, grated

2 tablespoons thick bottled mayonnaise

1 teaspoon snipped chives

2 tomatoes, thinly sliced

salt and freshly ground black pepper

4 small lettuce leaves

50 g/2 oz Danish Blue cheese, thinly sliced

75 g/3 oz Edam cheese, thinly sliced

4 teaspoons sweet pickle

1 Cut 3 horizontal slits in each roll (see Preparation). Spread the layers with margarine.

2 Put the Leicester cheese in a bowl with the mayonnaise and chives. Beat well until thoroughly blended. Sprinkle the tomato slices with salt and plenty of black pepper.

3 Place a lettuce leaf on the bottom layer of each roll and top with the blue cheese slices, dividing them equally between the rolls.

4 Spread the Leicester cheese mixture on the middle layer of each roll. Arrange the Edam cheese and tomato slices on the final layer, topping the cheese and tomato with a teaspoonful of pickle. Press the top of each roll down lightly.

Cook's Notes

TIME
Preparation takes about 25 minutes.

VARIATIONS
Ring the changes using other cheeses: mild-flavoured Cheddar, Stilton and Double Gloucester, or Caerphilly, Blue Cheshire and Gouda make good combinations for this snack.

SERVING IDEAS
Wrapped individually in cling film, these cheesy-filled rolls make ideal picnic food.

●500 calories/2100 kj per roll

PREPARATION
To cut slits in each roll ready for filling:

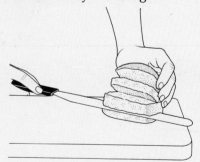

Slice through the roll horizontally, using a sharp knife and a sawing action. Do not cut right through the bread, the roll should be left 'hinged', to hold the filling and make the roll easier to eat.

Tasty cheese cakes

MAKES 8

100 g/4 oz **Red Leicester or Cheshire cheese, coarsely grated**

100 g/4 oz **mature Cheddar cheese, finely grated**

25 g/1 oz **margarine or butter**
1 small **onion, very finely chopped**
150 g/5 oz **fresh white breadcrumbs**
½ teaspoon **dried thyme**
100 g/4 oz **cottage cheese**
salt and freshly ground black pepper
2 **eggs, beaten**
2 tablespoons **chopped fresh parsley**
vegetable oil, for frying

GARNISH
8 small **gherkins, halved**
8 **stuffed olives, halved**

1 Melt the margarine in a frying-pan. Add the onion and fry gently for 5 minutes until soft and lightly coloured. Remove from the pan with a slotted spoon and cool on absorbent paper.

2 In a bowl, mix the grated cheeses with 75 g/3 oz of the breadcrumbs, the thyme, cottage cheese, and salt and pepper to taste. Add two-thirds of the egg and mix thoroughly.

3 Divide the mixture into 8 and shape each portion into a flat round cake. Refrigerate for 30 minutes (see Cook's tip).

4 Mix the remaining egg with 1 teaspoon of cold water in a shallow bowl. Mix the remaining breadcrumbs with the parsley, salt and pepper and spread out on a flat plate.

5 Coat the cakes in the egg, then in the breadcrumb mixture. ✳

6 Heat about 1 cm/½ inch of oil in a frying-pan until it is hot enough to turn a stale bread cube golden in 50 seconds. Add the cakes to the pan and fry for 2-3 minutes on each side until browned. [!] Drain well on absorbent paper.

7 Serve at once, garnished with gherkin and olive halves.

Sweet and sour sandwiches

SERVES 4

8 slices medium sliced brown bread
4 slices medium sliced white bread
margarine or butter, for spreading
100 g/4 oz Cheddar cheese, finely
  grated
1½ teaspoons French mustard
2 teaspoons Worcestershire sauce
175 g/6 oz stoned dates, chopped
1 tablespoon clear honey
2 tablespoons thick bottled
  mayonnaise
1 large eating apple, unpeeled,
  cored and finely chopped
4 large gherkins, thinly sliced

1 Spread margarine thinly on one side of all the slices of bread.
2 In a bowl mix the cheese, mustard and Worcestershire sauce with a fork, working the ingredients together to form a thick paste.
3 In a separate bowl mix together the dates, honey, mayonnaise and apple.
4 Spread the date and apple mixture on 4 slices of the brown bread. Top with the white slices, margarine side down.
5 Spread the top side of the white bread with margarine then spread cheese mixture on top of each slice.
6 Divide the gherkins between the 4 slices. Then cover with the remaining slices of brown bread.
7 Remove the crusts and cut the sandwiches into triangles to serve.

Gingered aubergine dip

SERVES 4

1 kg/2 lb firm aubergines, stems removed
175 ml/6 fl oz natural yoghurt
1 clove garlic, crushed (optional)
1 tablespoon light soft brown sugar
1 teaspoon grated fresh root ginger
½ teaspoon cumin powder
salt and freshly ground black pepper
fresh coriander or parsley sprigs, to garnish (optional)

1 Heat the oven to 200C/400F/Gas 6. Prick the aubergines all over with a fork, then put them into a roasting tin and bake in the oven for 45-60 minutes, until they feel really soft when they are pressed with the back of a spoon.

2 Remove the aubergines from the oven and leave until cool enough to handle. Cut them in half lengthways, and squeeze gently in your hand to drain off the bitter juices (see Preparation). Scoop out flesh and leave until cold.

3 Put aubergine flesh in a blender with the yoghurt, the garlic, if using, sugar, ginger, cumin and salt and pepper to taste. Blend until smooth. Transfer to 1 large or 4 small serving dishes. Refrigerate for 2-3 hours to allow dip to firm up.

4 Just before serving, garnish with coriander or parsley sprigs, if liked.

Cook's Notes

TIME
Preparing and cooking 1¼ hours, plus chilling.

SERVING IDEAS
Serve the dip with small pieces of toasted pitta bread and raw vegetables, such as carrot and cucumber sticks, strips of red and green pepper, tomato wedges, lengths of celery and cauliflower florets.

● 65 calories/275 kj per portion

PREPARATION
To extract the aubergine juices:

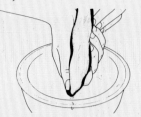

Hold the halved aubergines over a dish and squeeze gently in your hand so that the juices run out.

Autumn salad

SERVES 4
3 dessert apples (see Buying guide)
1 onion, thinly sliced and separated
    into rings
425 g/15 oz can butter beans,
    drained
50 g/2 oz walnut pieces
sprigs of mint, to garnish

DRESSING
150 g/5 oz natural yoghurt
1 tablespoon chopped mint
2 teaspoons lemon juice
salt and freshly ground black pepper

1 Make the dressing: mix yoghurt, mint and lemon juice in a large bowl and season to taste with salt and pepper.
2 Quarter, core and thinly slice the apples and then toss them in the yoghurt dressing until well coated.
3 Add the onion, butter beans and walnuts to the bowl and toss together. Turn the salad into a serving bowl, garnish with mint and serve at once.

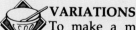

Cook's Notes

TIME
This refreshing salad takes only 20 minutes to prepare and dress.

BUYING GUIDE
To give the salad some colour, choose a red-skinned apple such as Red Delicious or Worcester.

VARIATIONS
To make a more substantial lunch dish, add 50 g/2 oz diced ham or cheese to the salad.
    For a different dressing, use mayonnaise instead of yoghurt and double the lemon juice.

● 190 calories/800 kj per portion

Index